PHILOSOPHY OF
COACHING

PHILOSOPHY OF COACHING

Over 100 Major Considerations to Improve Your Coaching Philosophy

By

LES LEGGETT

Department of Physical Education
University of Vermont
Burlington, Vermont

With Illustrations By

Shamms Mortier

CHARLES C THOMAS • PUBLISHER
Springfield • Illinois • U.S.A.

Published and Distributed Throughout the World by

CHARLES C THOMAS • PUBLISHER

2600 South First Street

Springfield, Illinois, 62717, U.S.A.

© *1983 by* CHARLES C THOMAS • PUBLISHER

ISBN 0-398-04784-7

Library of Congress Catalog Card Number: 82-16918

With THOMAS BOOKS *careful attention is given to all details of
manufacturing and design. It is the Publisher's desire to present books that
are satisfactory as to their physical qualities and artistic possibilities and
appropriate for their particular use. THOMAS BOOKS will be true to those
laws of quality that assure a good name and good will.*

Printed in the United States of America

I-R-1

Library of Congress Cataloging in Publication Data

Leggett, Les.
    Philosophy of coaching.

    Bibliography: p.
    1. Coaching (Athletics) I. Title.
GV711.L43   1983   796'.07'7   82-16918
ISBN 0-398-04784-7

PREFACE

A coaching philosophy that is based on sound values is perhaps the most essential ingredient for the successful coach. However, recorded information is not readily available.

From the researchers, we find attempts to list values acquired in sport and perhaps some hints as to how they may be found through some direct experience.

From the practitioners, or from those lifetime coaches who relate their experiences, comes much less information in this area. However, coaches do relate on a one-to-one basis all through their active coaching life. They discuss what happens and project "why." This seems to be the mode of communication of the average coach.

The following content is from a practitioner. The way it is presented is much as the average coach exchanges ideas. It is hoped that the beginning coach can benefit and that this book will offer a beginning for discussion for coaches with similar but often different experiences.

INTRODUCTION

A Record of What Was Learned

THE following pages are a summary of my coaching experiences that span nearly three decades. I recorded my thoughts after practices and contests and later categorized them. Reviewing the daily ledgers, I found that the majority of my recordings related to coach-athlete relationships, values, and coaching philosophy. My coaching experiences were in programs at the high school and small and medium-sized college levels. I hope that coaches in similar settings, as well as future coaches, will find much that is relevant in the pages ahead.

Why This Approach Was Chosen

As a lifelong teacher of kinesiology and physiology of exercise, I greatly value the need for the proper application of science in sport. It is a vital consideration. There are many other areas also vital to success, including game analysis, managerial talent, administrative and financial expertise, and surely the application of psychology. I will touch on all of these areas, but because it seemed the best way to group my daily entries, I have categorized the material as developed and applied philosophy. The objective of this book is to add to the reader's philosophy in areas that relate to successful coaching.

The coach, as an educator, has to be committed to a just philosophy and to improving the quality of life for students engaged in sport. The values in athletics play a vital supportive role to the goals of education. The values so easily achieved in sport become part of the athlete for life. They are a great return for his relatively brief exposure to a sport. His learned traits, habits, and values are often passed on to those with whom he deals. Who knows how far-reaching and widespread the ultimate result? The coach's charge goes beyond building skills and experiencing team success. His ultimate goal is to develop the full potential of the individual, to create the best possible product as a result of the athletes' participation. Texts seem to be lacking in this area.

It is also my belief that one of the greatest needs of the past, present, and future is the individual's need to improve values. The quality of one's life, and of all life on earth, depends on the kind of value judgments that are made in planning, reacting to crises, and in day-to-day relationships with others. The application of values in planning, reacting to problems, and in day-to-day relationships is the format of this text. A sound philosophy adds much to the "art" of working with athletes toward a common goal, and I strongly believe it is the most essential ingredient in coaching.

If one reviews the literature on coaching, one finds another strong justification for the title, *Philosophy of Coaching.* Most coaching texts emphasize techniques related to a particular sport, with a well-known coach as the author. Often, too, they stress general areas such as conditioning, budgeting, buying and caring for equipment, and practice organization. Topic coverage may be unique to a particular situation. What I have written is perhaps closely related to psychology of coaching literature. Although an instructor of a psychology of coaching course often deals in a more individualistic and specific problem approach, one could well adopt for discussion much of the content of this text. The art of coaching is using broad philosophical concepts in a skillful way to enhance the ultimate goal — to produce a better athlete and a better person. The approach is intended to be very broad. An instructor or reader will draw on specific personal experiences related to the concepts of each topic.

A Special Difficulty of This Task - The Discussion of Values

Values are difficult to discuss. "Values are abstract ideals . . ."[1]

---

[1] Reuben B. Frost, *Development of Human Values Through Sports.* Proceedings of national conference held at Springfield College, Springfield, Massachusetts, October 12-14, 1973 (Washington, D.C.: American Alliance for Health, Physical Education, and Recreation, 1974), p. 6.

"When we refer to human values we think of those attitudes and behaviors which emphasize and enhance the dignity and worth of man and his capacity for self-realization."[2]

Consideration for others, the spirit of empathy, fair play, graciousness in victory, respect for opponents, freedom to move, loyalty to teammates, giving of self, sincerity, justice, compassion, humility, respect, and honor are examples of attitudes and behaviors found in sport that contribute to ideals or values. "Those who have identified the values worth perpetuating as well as those values still to be identified and fostered will be the true leaders in sports, recreation, and physical education."[3]

We know that words often mean different things to different people, and values are less tangible than words. These combined facts hamper communication. Values may come forth as simple gut feelings on up to principles, upon which everything is built. Direct action in one's life results from great strength in certain values. Can we say that we have an important task ahead, but also a very difficult one?

One makes himself vulnerable when discussing values, as every reader has a different personal, playing, and coaching experience. Since most of the topics are open to debate, perhaps the material could be used in coaching classes as a comprehensive topic outline for discussion. I feel comfortable whenever I review a controversial topic. It could well be that my values would be different if my exposures had been different. Cherished values could change. One may well compare the text material to the role of discipline and appreciate the need for flexibility and review of judgment. I feel strongly, however, that my experiences were typical of many others in coaching. The topics discussed are typical of conversation when coaching friends get together.

Outline of Text

Little attention is given to the specific day-to-day administrative details of the job. Most details of administration are unique to

---

[2]Frost, p. 5.

[3]Edward J. Sims, *Development of Human Values Through Sports.* Proceedings of national conference held at Springfield College, Springfield, Massachusetts, October 12-14, 1973 (Washington, D.C.: American Alliance for Health, Physical Education, and Recreation, 1974), p. 8.

any situation. Much of the material covered is typical coach-to-coach daily office discussion. What was included in one heading may well have been included under another. It all depends on how one looks at the main issue. All headings, however, involve a philosophical consideration of coaching.

I have tried to avoid the typical textbook approach for two reasons. First, I am a practitioner, as are so many others in the field. The ideas are generated from typical personal experiences. It is the "way of a coach."

Second, much of coaching is an art. It seems appropriate to be informal. Coaching is value oriented. Coaching is dealing successfully with human and environmental variability. Coaches, for the most part, are so busy that they, too, have to be practitioners each day to survive.

There will be some repetition, as some thoughts will come through various ways throughout the text. Further, the thoughts on athletes were recorded over a long period of time, and some naturally will relate again to others. Some repetition is purposely included to emphasize what was learned.

Broad questions are included at the end of each brief topic to help the reader review and expand on what was covered. If the book is used as a classroom text, the discussion leader may use the broad outline of topics and expand the questions and assign other related work. Whatever the reader's position — prospective coach or experienced coach — content is set forth informally, relating to incidents, and in common coaching lingo with hopes of making reading a relevant and enjoyable experience.

CONTENTS

PHILOSOPHY OF COACHING

Chapter 1

TO COACH OR NOT,
OR HOW DO YOU MEASURE UP?

WHY COACH?

PERHAPS one asks this question before any other. The answer
may be simple for the beginner. "I want to coach so that I
can teach the sport(s) I know well to others and have them gain
the kinds of good experiences that I had as an athlete." This reason
is sufficient for the beginning coach and possibly the experienced
coach. If ego to prove that you can win is a strong motivator, then
again, you may be somewhat typical.

You will have to look at things a bit differently as time goes by, however, to be the kind of coach that has it all together. The older coach continues because more each year he seems to value the relationships he has with the youngsters. They are like his own. Each youngster has strengths, and the coach is trying to find them and help the athlete gain confidence by using his assets. A primary goal is to get the best physical and mental performance possible, but an equal satisfaction is observing a youngster's physical, mental, and spiritual strengths develop and mature off the field. This reward that comes to the coach is what makes him live out another year. The young coach may live throughout the season's wars and poor coaching situations to satisfy his ego's need for wins. The older coach has gone through the seasons many times. He knows his competition and realizes he will probably get only so much success scorewise, depending on the native talent and the hard work put into the season. He is conditioned for 150 percent effort and for whatever comes, and he is on sound ground. If you put all of your eggs into one basket and only your ego to win is involved, losses after all your efforts will make you discouraged, and wins will give you a false sense of your worth. If you are working hard, enjoying each athlete as you go, the wins and losses balance according to talent, and you'll have great rewards — regardless of how any uninformed fan may judge you as a result of your season's record. Mediocrity is not advocated here, just realism. One may never get over some ties and one point losses, but over the long haul if you are well prepared, you will have your share of elations, too. With the right attitude about teaching outcomes in athletics, the key to successful coaching, you will be "successful" regardless of what uphill situation you are in. If more coaches looked at their coaching this way, there would be more older coaches around.

One might also sum up coaching in this way: *it is giving of yourself,* your energies, knowledge, special talents in sport, and most of all your wisdom, *to the athletes and to your common goals.*

The following by an unknown author sums it up quite well:

We give of ourselves
  When we give *gifts of the heart:*
   love, kindness, joy, understanding,
    sympathy, forgiveness.

We give of ourselves
  when we give *gifts of the mind:*
   ideas, dreams, purposes, ideals, principles,
    plans, inventions, projects, poetry.

We give of ourselves
  when we give the *gift of time:*
   patience, attention, consideration.

We give of ourselves
  when we give the *gift of words:*
   encouragement, inspiration, guidance.

The finest gift a man can give to his age and time
  is the gift of a constructive and creative life.

The mature coach looks at his job as a spiritual commitment to people and a good cause. He has to be totally involved. He has to get others to want to be led by him. He has to live by "The Art of Giving" to do this. *He is evaluated by his dedication, judgments, knowledge, and enthusiasm. What the coach is as a human being is perhaps the most important of all assets.* Even the very young can not only sort out truth and falsehood but they can go far beyond this in evaluating their coach. If your peers respect you for what you do and what you are and like being with you, then you should be a good candidate for maturing as a coach.

Are there other reasons to enter coaching?
What are your reasons?

DEMANDS

Demands on the coach make his job quite unique. Time demands alone make it an almost unreasonable position. The coach's job is also many faceted — each aspect adds or detracts from his goals. Whatever the coaching situation, he is under pressures. He knows that in the final analysis a coach is often judged by his record. It may be outside pressure to win. Pressure to win solely from within is always there. He wants to do his very best and he knows what above and beyond effort is. He expects a lot from his athletes and wants to put more into the season than the most dedicated of them. He must lead by displaying the greatest effort of all. His goal, because of the scheduling odds, could only be to win enough so as to keep his program in respectability. This is pressure, too. The coach also has pressure on him continually to never be outcoached. A loss resulting from a mistake on his part is something that takes a lot of time to get over. In some situations, there is also pressure to satisfy the top echelon of athlete. He is super serious, as you are, and his need must be met. Your program should challenge the most talented. Parents can provide pressure, too. Each parent is unique when it comes to his child, and his pursuits. You have to satisfy in every way. Fans also are sometimes very unreasonable. You are motivated from all sides to provide a better all-around atmosphere, as well as to meet your competition. The 8:00 a.m. to 5:00 p.m. job is out.

It has been said that a successful coach should be able to confine his time demands to just two things — his job and his family. The person that has a lot of interests wants to do other things with some of his time. He may, therefore, devote less time to his work over the long haul and quite possibly be less efficient in some areas. It is good, however, for a coach to have other interests. It may make for a more rounded person, and there is definitely a great need for more well-rounded teachers and coaches. A broad background offers more opportunities to relate to a wide variety of individuals. Another reason that a coach benefits from many interests is that his world can never completely crumble because all of his eggs are not in one basket. Life is in better perspective. In addition, by having other long-term interests, one may be gearing oneself for the long-term, which is a real need in coaching. Too many coaches give so much of themselves that they get enough of it in early life. Regardless of your makeup, there is a large segment of your professional life that has to have a special concentrated emphasis and a time commitment. Weekends added on to long hours during the midweek tend to consume the coach.

Peter Daland, in talking about coaching demands in an *American Swim Coaches Newsletter,* states,

> If you have family obligations, it is going to be tough. You are going to have to decide where your priorities are. There is a very high divorce rate in coaching, not because of immorality, but because of extreme pressure on coaching people. If you're an age group coach working with an AAU Club, in all probability you are going to have to give up over half the weekends of the year, all day Saturday and all day Sunday. If you are married to someone who doesn't like that, you have a decision to make before your partner makes the decision for you. That is a very big problem. I really feel that swimming today is asking too much of coaches. I think the program we are running is right training-wise, but very wrong competition-wise. All-day meets, half the weekends of the year, is not the way to run swimming, it's the way to run divorce. It is a terrible thing for the family life of coaches. I think it's the wrong way to run this sport. Also, it eventually wipes out swimmers and parents. I'm speaking in favor of doing something that will save swimming and the people in swimming.

About any sport finds the coach caught up in being as competitive as he has to be to survive and have some success. Each year, coaching, like many other fields, gets more specialized and demands more of those involved.

What can you add to this topic?

WHAT IS SUCCESS?

Success in the scheme of life might be summed up as follows:

> That man is a success
> who has lived well,
> laughed often and loved much;
> Who has gained the respect
> of intelligent men
> and the love of children;
> Who has filled his niche
> and accomplished his task;
> Who leaves the world better
> than he found it,
> Whether being an improved poppy,
> a perfect poem,

or rescued a soul;
Who never lacked appreciation
of earth's beauty
or failed to respect it;
Who looked for the best in others
and gave the best he had.

Author Unknown

Perhaps in a broad sense there is nothing left to say. However, in the narrower sense of a coaching career, what are elements that indicate success?

Just as there are many kinds of athletes that are successful, so are there just as many different approaches to success in coaching. Experiences for this writer were in situations where the coach was also a part of the faculty. In other words, academic teaching was definitely a large part of the load. Surely these kinds of institutions provide a common emphasis on athletic programs, and in various parts of the country where I taught and coached, I found a variation in the way things were done. To gain a grasp of the exact feelings of the athlete is the key, and this factor varies bacause of many reasons. To set forth a formula for success in broad terms is perhaps the only attempt one can make to evaluate success. The combinations of assets are infinite for success just as they are for successful family living. If the good qualities outweigh the bad, then is one judged successful? Perhaps, but what is the weight to what qualities? Just as volumes can be written on the mental training of the athlete, a great deal of a coach's success is related to his inspirational ability as expressed in many forms. Just as an athlete's success may be 90 percent related to his mind, then so it is with the coach and how he uses his personality, character, and ability to create confidence to get others to work towards the common goal; this premise could relegate less percentage to the technical. The ideal coach is not only a very good organizer, technician, etc., but is also a good public relations man, with a super ability to get youngsters to understand what to do and have them develop great dedication. The more the coach has going for him as a person, the better are his chances for success.

To go a bit further in trying to evaluate who is the successful coach, one might begin by observing how the athletes look at him when they are in a tough losing situation. Is he still their leader? If he is in charge, then he has made it on contest administration and as a technician, as well as as an individual they respect.

A coach can be successful if he has a great respect from and good relationship with the athletes. He might not be the best technician in the world, but he cannot be successful if he does not have the athletes with him.

The innate patterns possessed by the coach such as his drive, approach to things, and personality all may not change much so they need to be present in an appealing package to begin with. Why? Because he is a sum total of all his past experiences and is now pretty much established as far as the way he deals with people. A person is often somewhat mature, stable, and predictable at the age of the beginning coach. The perfection of teaching, his knowledge, and his game administration, which are all very important, are perhaps not yet all together, and if this is tackled with strong motivation, eventually he will feel master of his field. He can still be a successful coach, then, if he is only on his way in this latter department. Perhaps a statement by the late Vince Lombardi summed up the learning venture when he said that "leadership or teachership is not so much leading as having the people led, accept you. You know how you do that; you've got to win the hearts of the people you lead. The *personality* of the individual has to do with it."

You must win the athlete over by your dedication, personality, and ability to put things together. To gain a grasp on his effort by motivating him is the art and science of coaching. Lombardi's philosophy worked in the pros and it seems to support my feelings about this kind of approach in the educational athletic picture.

How do you define success?

REWARDS

Many coaching situations are not financially rewarding. In some situations, however, the coach's role is recognized as a very demanding and important job, and he is rewarded in proportion. Mistake number one is to enter the field with ideas that it is generally lucrative on most high school and college levels. Rationale could easily be provided to justify why the superior coach should be awarded top salary. Unfortunately, not all administrators fully appreciate the dedication and outcomes involved in coaching.

Fortunately, the coach's rewards are far more reaching and lasting than money. It's not only the most demanding but the most rewarding job in the whole educational picture. It is even more rewarding to many, myself included, than the role of directing and possibly creating outstanding programs. The satisfactions come directly to you from the youngsters with whom you share so much. The dealings are intense, personal, and the lifetime ties are forever there for the coach and athlete — you gain new family each year. The coach sees the changes in the athlete that he helped create. The camaraderie can be an overwhelming and lasting reward. I don't know where it could be greater. Up front and coaching is where " it's at."

Every year or two, an athlete may voluntarily say, "This was the most important experience I have had while in school." What a compliment. Recognition by outside groups and parents is a frequent reward of the coach, too.

That a group may voluntarily get together to financially contribute hard to come by funds to show appreciation for the coaches' effort is another impressive testimony to the rewards of coaching. Being a classroom teacher, as well as a coach, I can say with confidence that you will have to live through quite a few years to find a group of youngsters getting involved to the extent that it occurs in athletics. An excellent teacher, in his lifetime, may not experience the one year satisfactions of a coach. This is a heavy statement but one I believe I can make with authority. It would be great to see classroom teaching take on the intensity, general student support, and significance in the lives of students that athletics achieves. It's a challenge for teaching — a challenge that is actually realistic. It would require as a number one prerequisite that teachers attacked their roles with the vigor a coach has to assume. The coach's work is periodically on display, and the feedback is often quite instant, as are the satisfactions in seeing your efforts materialize. It is not the intention to degrade classroom teaching. However, coaching is more competitive — the average and poor coaches get relieved.

Are there other rewards?

THE FUTURE

There are many changes taking place in the educational picture. In public education alone, the financial picture dictates that physical education, and athletics in particular, will have more monetary problems in the foreseeable future. Already, finances are a real problem. Many coaches and teachers are leaving the field for better paying positions. It is conceivable that only the most dedicated will remain along with some that are fortunate just to keep their jobs. In many situations, the prevailing trends will hurt educational outcomes. However, teachers and the coaches are the real forces that hold programs together.

The coach may well see the need to direct more effort into fund raising in order to maintain viable programs. One may object, philosophically, to a coach having to raise some of his own funds. However, if fund raising is done right, it can bring the group closer together and teach them many valuable lessons. Perhaps among the foremost of appreciations is the value of money. The ways are endless to earn supporting funds. Any resourceful person can discover what is best for his or her situation. Thus, no need for my long list of ways to supplement budgets. You are limited only by your situation and imagination.

Aside from the tax dollars being more limited in your athletic program, the energy problem is here to stay. The cost of fuel will affect some teams that have schedules requiring a lot of distance travel. In many sections of the country, this could present quite a problem. The energy costs also are reflected in costs of motels. Food prices are affected because of transportation costs. It is an endless chain related to energy. Inflation's costs of all kinds are directly related. Aside from available supporting funds, the inflation syndrome is going to place some limitations on what support can be given to sports activities. If travel is about 80 percent of a budget, anyone can predict a problem in the future.

Next, the lack of publicity in some sports will hurt them. There are so many other sports in the curriculum now — nearly double that of just a few years ago — that there is just not enough room for all to have proper media coverage. You may be hurt by what the sports writers have to emphasize or just what they want to emphasize. At any rate, support publicity will not often go to the most deserving. The media really does have quite an influence on what has happened and what will happen in sport, unfortunately perhaps, but true. The media often reflects demand, and possibly just as frequently, it reflects a writer's personal interests.

Many sports will lose following, and this in turn will affect the athlete's motivation, accomplishment, and discipline: a real negative. The author has experienced good publicity and poor publicity. There was a time when much space was devoted in the local paper to swimming, which changed to a time of nearly nothing. *Example:* An All-American assistant coach was added to the staff, and the school media had a low priority on reporting of the sport and would only report his school and year of graduation with no personal mention of his athletic honors. Poor judgment? A writer's prejudice? That's seeing it all from great to "zilch."

There are other problems related to the increased demands on coaches and teachers. Having additional jobs, being spread too thin, once again is often related to money available. Emphasis as well as the consequent values attained will be affected. Coaching has many innate problems and does not need more serious obstacles.

A coach is just a person, and no matter how much he likes his work, adding more roles, such as fund raising, to the load can hurt his long-term enthusiasm. A person gets tired of too much work regardless of how enjoyable the heavy load may be.

Being split, like working for athletics and physical education, is a natural combination. However, it often is quite awkward trying to satisfy two bosses, especially so if one administrator does not appreciate the time spent with your other half load. Thus, one is split even further. Even with positive administrative support, performing a dual or multiple role creates problems in evaluation. Each segment often suffers because efforts are less than full time in each. The evaluator has to understand that he is evaluating only part-time effort — a hard thing to do. It is a situation that changes and can become a real problem in some instances.

On the plus side, sport is as old as man. Youngsters will keep things going. The coach's leadership will become more important for the aforementioned difficulties. The coach may just have to take on more outside assignments. In our country, we demand a seriousness and a dedication in sport, and therefore there will always be a need for fine coaches.

We also have a present trend that notes many people of all ages seeking physical activity. This has been a result of media rather than what was learned in outstanding programs. A much needed "plus" for the media. Regardless, it is good to have many community members more conscious of the physical development of the individual. Possibly there will emerge a more appreciative attitude concerning physical education and athletics. It is a great time to emphasize the involvement of the community in fitness programs.

When we can do as well in international competition as we do, regardless of the comparison of the numbers of people and rewards involved, it surely is a tribute to the all-around situation we have in our country. Genuine intrinsic motivation has to be a great factor. There is no question that with greater outside funding and governmental support, our country could greatly improve our present position as well as promote a more homogenous and nationalistic spirit. You may be going into a more difficult situation than that of your past classmates. However, your field is still fertile. Good people are needed for the future. The coach of the future will be better prepared than his counterpart of the past. The coach of the future will face more problems, and will also be in a more competitive situation.

What do you feel your future position, five years from now, will reflect?

What trends would you project for the distant future?

How will an increase in specialization affect sport on your level?

LIKING PEOPLE

Almost everyone likes people. Let's take a safe position and say that this expression is shown in degrees. The topic is discussed because I have observed happy and unhappy people in the field. Perhaps it is more than happy versus unhappy. When a teacher or coach commonly displays a sharp retort to a youngster for something trivial, I wonder if that person should be around youngsters. Certainly they are not establishing any great bonds between each, as evidenced by the observable communication, and it is clear that the coach is not enjoying his work. It is true that this quality could be related to temporary personal problems, being too busy, etc., and possibly the older person under pressure is a bit less patient. However, if negativism is an ongoing characteristic of the leader's behavior, then there is a question whether that person is accomplishing his role. Does the coach enjoy being around youngsters a good part of his working day? There are some situations like the "winning at all costs" that also have made less friendly, less tolerant beings out of coaches. Some teaching situations are truly at fault for the "psychotic" teacher. Just having to do too many diverse things is a prime example. Poor school and family discipline is another factor related to coach-athlete relationships. A coach, regardless of the factors mentioned, must convey a "liking people" relationship that is genuine.

The teaching situation for you is one where you can go to your practice with the attitude that you are looking forward to seeing the young athletes enjoying their youth and to observe them enthusiastically tackling their outlined tasks. A coach can work just as hard and be just as good if he is a youngster at heart. Looking forward to having some fun at practice might be contrasted to the coach dreading the hard work to come or who is just too serious with his approach.

The successful older coach has more pure enjoyment in his dealings with youngsters. His younger years may have been more pressured by a common desire to establish himself — to win his share. The old coach that has had many fulfillments is perhaps in a better position to enjoy a more philosophical approach — one advantage of lasting a while. The later years *can* be more rewarding.

How much do I really enjoy people — youngsters — is perhaps a first priority question for the young coach to ask himself.

Perhaps it would be helpful to expand on this topic and develop a coaching fitness test.

JUSTIFYING SALARY

Because communities cannot "afford" more taxes, townspeople are apt to be more critical of budgets and of their teachers and coaches. If the teaching-coach is seen downtown too early in the day or is observed to have time in the summer, then it is easy to question the salary of that faculty member.

The time/energy factor needs to be clarified. The way I looked at my life as a teacher and coach is that a year's work is condensed into a school year period. To put two school years together back to back would be impossible for me and many others. If enthusiasm and good productivity are important, one needs time to "heal." You will be with youngsters from early morning to late evening plus weekends. There are even stretches of months at a time when you will never be away a full day from some of your students. Your job never ends; it just lasts longer during the school year and even longer during the season you coach.

The following is a typical account of what teacher-coach is expected to do:

The day may begin with your arrival at school at seven in the morning to meet cheerfully the group of youngsters under your direct responsibility. You have to generate enthusiasm regardless of how you feel. The constant display of enthusiasm may drain your energies, but you are their teacher and your job is to encourage them in their work. You continue on into the late evenings to keep up with homework assignments, reading up-to-date information, and correcting papers. Your teaching must be top quality in every class or practice, or your only solace is to rededicate your efforts to having the very best class or practice the next day. Your personal satisfaction is a prime reward. On top of the normal routine, you must help wherever you are needed. It may be driving a bus, selling candy at games, administering the yearbook, taking orders for class rings, supervising hot lunch, monitoring study hall, and working with student organizations. Above all, you are mindful of always spreading enthusiasm and never losing patience. You have to communicate your goals and relate them to those of the students and athletes. The coach has pressures on him from students who need many things and from parents who want many things — often unreasonable. So the coach tries to be on top for every need, and in between, he has to line the field, clean the locker rooms, lay out equipment, and check on the schedule of contests to be sure all details are covered. He has to check officials and other help, pay them, handle traffic control, spectator's program, the halftime entertainment, and on and on, depending on the size of the institution. The larger school actually has less nitty gritty but more to delegate — either one is about as demanding.

Perhaps the breaks in details are taken up with your treatment of discipline problems — trying to terminate all dealings in the most fair and satisfactory way. You are the expert in handling people, and you are ever preparing to do a better job of individualizing what you and the student do.

After a typical day of being trainer, first aider, and following up on any injuries at odd hours, you have not forgotten to order your equipment, have the physicals scheduled at the proper time, get your parent permission forms in on file, and call ahead for making meal arrangements or have your manager draw the necessary funds for the trip. Then you arrive home late that evening after a contest. More of the same next day, next weekend. Try putting a couple of seasons and school years back to back and the community will need to find another replacement. No other city employee has such a diverse assignment and often is appreciated less. An assignment that takes a never ending preparation. An assignment that demands so much extra time with youngsters, with their well-being as a foremost concern. The public has a great buy — hardly a dollar an hour to the expert for the contact time the teacher-coach has with their youngsters after school hours. The community has entrusted you with their child, and many voters do not realize that society depends on the school's proper guidance in good values and the best in learning situations. It is just expected.

One could just think about all the work and crises and get discouraged. But remember that any position in the world is only as good as you make it. You will make your own rewards — giving them to yourself when you know you did a super job, and you will take them away when you know you did not. You will be most fortunate if you have a boss that compliments you on a good job. The top flight administrator knows the value of encouragement to staff development and morale. What someone else gives you, they can take away — so forget it. You will become strong, resourceful, self-reliant, and mature by the nature of your work, which is a reward in itself. The best reward of all is seeing a youngster mature into a real, successful person and knowing that you played an important role in all this development.

Executives often have diverse jobs; calling meetings to solve problems is common. The coach oftentimes has no one to meet with and no time to meet. He cannot call a committee together. He has to make the decisions, good or bad, often in dramatic fashion, and live with the outcomes. This is what the coaching minicrisis demands. Having to "fly by the seat of your pants" develops the art of coaching. Yes, the teacher-coach is worth his salary by the following criteria alone. Just multiply the contact hours by number of students exposure.

There is no other setting that can duplicate the role of the teacher-coach. Other than the family setting, the youngsters spend the next greatest block of time in school and related settings. The teacher-coach is entrusted to enhance each individual's growth, growth that in many ways is not possible at home or in any other setting.

Are you prepared to defend to local citizens your educational role and salary?

Perhaps the administrators should justify why they offer so little for so much?

THE KEY JOB

The job of a coach is to take the athlete as he is, with what he may believe in as a personal philosophy, change only what is changeable, and completely accept him as a package. If the athlete feels at ease with you because you genuinely accept him, then you have him on your side. He has accepted you. Having the athlete fit a mold is not the way to the best coach-athlete relationship. If coaches are honest with themselves, they must admit that they were also different at times in their younger years. Like many other respected humans, they are what they are but for a fine line and the grace of God.

A coach has an image of what an athlete ought to be. This is important. Sometimes other great qualities are overlooked because the athlete lacks a special quality — personal appearance. The coach refuses to deal person to person until the athlete has submitted to the coach's ideal. This is a double standard. The coach respects his other colleagues — say a fellow professor with his shabby appearance — and yet is harder on a youngster trying to find a personal special identity. Accept the athlete for what he is to you and what he is as a person, and he will accept you regardless of your looks or idiosyncrasies. The caring bond is now open for both parties to enjoy.

The above paragraph does not negate or de-emphasize a coach's goal of having the best possible team and individual *image*. The coach just has to know when to forget some things in favor of keeping top level communication and mutual faiths.

If you were to expand this topic, what would you list as a coach's next most important factor?

THE RAW COMPONENT

To sort out the important things that would be of help to the beginning coach, "hard work" would have to be near the top of the list. George Bernard Shaw put it this way, "When I was a young man, I observed that nine out of ten things I did were failures. I didn't want to be a failure, so I did ten times more work." When the "boss" works hard, so does the crew. The loafing boss *does not* have loyal and hard working staff.

If you put in enough hours and do things right, you are going a long way to improve every quality of performance. You are motivating others by just your being. By your total immersion and commitment, you are attracting more athletes that are serious about their efforts. You are creating a better environment for the team and for others to observe. You are showing organization, developing responsibility among the team, and offering the right kind of experiences to improve their education. What you do speaks for itself. They will sense your total commitment and will want to please you by living up to what you want done. The teachers and coaches I remember were those who were deeply committed to what they were doing. It will establish the bond and create the atmosphere you need to do the coaching job you want. It covers for a lot of mistakes, too. And no matter what one wants to think, mistakes are made in great numbers by the athlete, the officials, and the coach. To put it one other way — persistence will win for you every time. The problem many of you will have here is that you will be so spread out trying to do a good job in so many areas that you will be dissatisfied about your coaching job and teaching assignment as well.

Did the few outstanding teachers and coaches you remember have a deep commitment?

Where would you rate enthusiasm as the most vital component?

Hard work must have a well planned direction. Have you known coaches that could have been more successful if they could have been more efficient in applying their energy?

A CHALLENGE

One of the most glaring of all needs in the field of education and sport today is that there is inadequate financial support. However, *priorities* to adequately fund your area may also be lacking. Needs are clearly known and projected to the administration, and yet year after year these needs are not even partially met. It becomes very easy to give up, and many coaches in their older years do just that. However, the *challenge is to keep a professional attitude in light of getting shot down in nearly everything you ask.* It is easy to get gun shy and not continue to make the pitch for your needs. But those people in the system who have acquired what they asked for are those that have persisted with adequate justification and diplomacy.

Every school has its problems, and some schools have more than others. The challenge, to not gripe but just to go about your job, is certainly there. Most of the time, your program is what you make it. The coach makes it either a good one or one not so good.

What are other concerns and challenges for you?

THE IDEAL COACH

There is no one role model — great ones are found in many packages. What are some ingredients? As previously emphasized, a coach must be someone who likes other people and sees the fun and learning opportunities in human nature. In particular, he likes to be with the athlete. This is enjoyment to him. He likes sport and wants to teach all he knows about his sport to others. His ego is not an issue. The issues center around the responsibility to the athletes entrusted to him. Just as any culture needs common bonds, interests, and loyalties in order to be strong, a sports team needs to share among each member the common interests, loyalties, and goals.

I like the together approach for fostering closeness between coach and athlete. Surely, a coach could be great and perhaps would not subscribe to this area. However, I personally value that relationship. I also like to see the kind of coach that the athletes like being around. Athletes should be attracted to him or her as a person personifying their sex. Perhaps this denotes physical conditioning and living habits. It certainly is a broad area. Leadership, respect, inspiration, and communication go easily to the coach who is an example and who is close to his athletes because he enjoys his close relationships.

Ethics are an essential ingredient. If you ever win by a shady move it will always be remembered by your fellow coaches. It is essential to be strong and fair. Athletes at any age expect the right conduct and cannot be fooled. What is an example? How about the coach respecting the officials' decisions? The coach that saved his protests *until he knew he was right* would have far fewer contested situations in his lifetime. DePaul's Ray Meyer, a basketball Hall of Fame candidate and long-time coach can count on one hand the technical fouls called on him. Some coaches have received more infractions in one game. Coaches in pressure situations have the greatest confrontation with ethics.

A coach must fit into the school system that hires him. Every system is different, and all have their problems. The idea is to adopt their philosophy and be loyal. If you find it difficult to be loyal and enhance your school, then it is time to move to a different situation. The ideal coach fits the situation. He is compatible. This does not mean he is settling for mediocrity. He just takes sport as far as he can the right way.

The ideal coach gets along well in the community and with parents. He has a way with people. They are attracted to him. They support him. He says the right kinds of things. He is respected for all his dealings. People from the outside, as well as his athletes, feel comfortable with him. This goes for a lasting relationship.

There may be a host of suggestions concerning the ideal coach. I have listed a few key components that readily come to mind. Perhaps it would be very profitable to open this question to all athletes to see what they think as well as to inquire of other coaches. There is much room for the sharing of other experiences.

It should enhance your philosophy to make your own list of qualities that you, as the "ideal coach," want to possess.

WHAT KIND OF IMAGE?

When you begin your coaching career, there are a couple of things that often occur. First, you may employ a system of play and a routine of doing things learned from previous exposure. You are comfortable this way. You feel that past successes will follow. This is natural. Second, it is common for the new coach to *not* go beyond implementation of exposed systems of play. He may not yet be completely sure of himself, and he may act through his interpretation of what the coach that he played for would do or say. Though this is normal, one must be free from all of the above aspects to be on the right track. *The mature coach has to believe in his own reasons for using the routine and system he wants, and he must act through his own personality in solving all problems.* It takes some people years before they are truly their own person. In fact, the maturing process is lifelong. Coaching matures you faster than most other kinds of experiences because you are involved in a concentrated life, and youngsters' needs are always pressing. It takes a lifetime to reach the ultimate. The sooner you are able to develop your own image and reasons for your teachings, the sooner you will be "your own person." A coach has to reflect confidence and act accordingly. This comes at different rates to different people. When the above is achieved, the image projected will be natural and as it should be. The intent of this topic is to emphasize the aforementioned two major points.

This topic could also have covered personal living habits, as well as other related factors. However, acceptable variations can be applied from situation to situation. In this vein, however, the athletic image means clean living, respect for conditioning, hard work, and unquestionable ethics. Without having this going for you, regardless of where you are, you are lacking proper image.

What specifically have you noticed about some beginning coaches relative to image? What images can you relate concerning the master coach?

THE OUTSTANDING ATHLETE AS COACH

The athlete who was not a "natural" but was dedicated to learning all he could will know exactly what it is like to make mistakes. Therefore, he may be in a better position to coach than the natural athlete. The natural athlete often performs with expertise and ease. This may not help later when he coaches. He may not have had the learning problems of the average athlete. Therefore, he could be lacking in direct teaching experiences. An average skilled athlete who never had an outstanding day, but who had good, sound coaching and studied his sport, may have a better start on teaching his sport. The exposure of playing is where one gains the foundation to coach — not in the classroom. However, every day is a day for you or against you in that you have to constantly prove yourself. It is what one does each day to become the best that gets you there. So, if you are a good athlete with a good coach in your background, you should have the right start. A top-notch coaching exposure is equally vital to acquiring skills, regardless of ability. It is what the author likes to see for beginners. If you have worked hard as an athlete, not been outstanding in any way, but have the same burning desire, you may go far beyond the outstanding natural athlete, as leadership is in constant demand. A leader one day means very little the next.

It is also possible to be a good coach without yourself being a participant in the sport. The numbers are fewer. The road to "feeling" the fundamentals in mental movement patterns is harder. However, the would-be coach can learn by his exposures, whatever they are. If you can feel comfortable in your kinesiology background and basic fundamentals of sport and can get the athlete's confidence and desire to follow you, you have the necessary elements going for you. The greater number of sports activities in which you participate, the greater can be your adaptability in an unfamiliar sport.

The intent of this topic is not to downgrade the natural and outstanding athlete. The intent is to emphasize the possible strengths of the athlete who had to learn a harder way and to stress the importance of an exposure to excellent coaching.

What kind of athlete and learner were you?

How far does your desire to coach go back?

Did you have an outstanding coach in your life?

WHY DO COACHES FAIL?

One may take the position that coaches fail for many different reasons and combinations of reasons. Is there any one factor that dominates? A coach may get along well with administrators, faculty, peers, etc. A coach may seek excellence and demand that his goals be met. The coach can provide variety in workouts and can properly delegate tasks so that he can accomplish more important coaching functions. The coach may be a great organizer, a fine technician, and top-notch game administrator. The coach may keep up with the latest happenings in his/her sport. The coach may even have a fine personality, really "like" people. There are many other plusses a coach can have and *still fail.*

Having coached for nearly thirty years, I think of one factor as a key to success or failure time and again. Within one university, I once observed two coaches in one year fail because of a single and most vital *lack* — the "WE" approach. The athletes and coach both want to win, but how they want to go about it is different. Problems very often come from the coach and athlete not having the same day-to-day goals. When coaches fail, they lack proper communication between themselves and their athletes. With the "WE" approach, the coach can become flexible and patient. If the sport season is an "I" venture for the coach, he may be unresponsive to suggestions or even quite defensive. In either case, a breach in communication is occurring.

The coach is not harnessing strengths nor is the coach accepting each person as a person when suggestions are met with deaf ears or a negative response, such as words to the effect, "Are you questioning my ability as a coach?" The together position would promote a "Let's sit down and see where WE can be more effective." Oftentimes, the athlete's suggestions do not make a real contribution, but if the athlete is a part of the planning, he may work harder. The coach's ultimate daily reward is to observe a *hard day's work* — and to *also observe a happy athlete* as well.

The coach who draws away from suggestions is cutting off communication — instead of the athlete and coach drawing closer together, the poles are becoming farther apart. It is more difficult to observe that hard day's work and, also, the happy athlete. A coach cannot last long if he or she does not enter the practice and game as a joint, enthusiastic, fun, hard-working venture. To criticize athletes, not take suggestions, or become defensive is the beginning of another failing coach.

Coaches do not last a long time at best. The average tenure is perhaps around seven years. Losing situations (records) account for a lot of discouragement, *but* a lot of discouragement comes from the coach not realizing that he should approach each practice as a fun place to be and a place to talk individually with each athlete. He enjoys youth and is ever aware of opening communication along any level.

Rate your reactions to the following:

Positive	Negative	
_____	_____	1. How do you respond when an athlete or athletes come to you with a suggestion?
_____	_____	2. How do you react to a suggestion when you feel it is totally out of order?
_____	_____	3. How do you react to a suggestion that is very crudely and undiplomatically presented to you?
_____	_____	4. How do you react when your athletes lose?
_____	_____	5. How do you react after a contest when your athletes perform below your expectations?

Yes	No	
_____	_____	6. Do you really listen to your athletes as evidenced by a change in your behavior?
_____	_____	7. During a contest (playing time), your athletes may perform below your expectations. Do you openly or publicly react in a negative manner?
_____	_____	8. Can you criticize *your own* coaching when things do not go right?
_____	_____	9. Do you ever feel the squad performs poorly because of your inability to stress the needed skills?

Yes   No

_____   _____ 10. When a squad is unhappy, do you ever feel it may be because of *your* approach?

_____   _____ 11. Perhaps you are not having fun. Are you looking forward to the season's ending?

_____   _____ 12. Does it matter to you if your athletes are happy?

_____   _____ 13. Are you working hard to please your athletes?

_____   _____ 14. Are you sensitive to the athletes' feelings when you comment to the press or to others?

_____   _____ 15. Do you ever joke among coaches or to others about the hamburgers, red shirt group, etc.?

_____   _____ 16. Do you feel that your less talented athletes are poor athletes rather than just at different stages of development?

_____   _____ 17. Do you speak individually with each athlete every practice?

_____   _____ 18. Do you sit down off-season with each athlete and set goals and agree on how you'll both go about reaching these goals?

_____   _____ 19. Do you have personality conflicts with some athletes?

Reactions of the coach who is heading for problems:

1. Negative	10. No
2. Negative	11. No
3. Negative	12. No
4. Negative	13. No
5. Negative	14. No
6. No	15. Yes
7. Yes	16. Yes
8. No	17. No
9. No	18. No
	19. Yes

Chapter 2

THE SETTING

THE COACH AND HIS ASSISTANTS

IF a coach has an assistant(s), he is able to delegate part of the load to them. Assistant coaches add tremendously to the coaching position. An excellent assistant can share a great deal of the head coach's responsibilities. However, the head coach must know exactly just what to let others do and what not to do.

Perhaps the head coach should first put himself in the position of the assistant. The assistant will work hard if he feels he has a vital role and if he gets the rewards for his efforts. I have observed and participated in situations where the assistant was not given any real responsibility and authority to do a job and was not even allowed to get close to the athletes. This situation destroys initiative, and over a period of time, the enjoyment of giving of himself will be lacking for the assistant. To get a "bone" every once in a while and then have the role taken away is playing with another human being's sincerest efforts. It will not foster more hard work, loyalty, or a stronger organization. Further, head coaches should also realize that many assistants do not want to be a head coach, or do not at least want his job. A secure head coach is never challenged, and if an assistant has the strength, he should be given reasonable responsibility so that he can develop. This is the head coach's responsibility to another human being. The head coach will grow as well. You can never fool an athlete young or old. The head coach must always hold the assistants in highest esteem and readily give credit. I mention this above illustration as they are basic thoughts crossing the head coach's and assistant coach's mind and can play a healthy or unhealthy role in the organization.

The age of the head coach can be his greatest handicap. Until he is completely confident and secure, he will not be able to delegate responsibility efficiently. Also, a sheer age difference alone is an experience edge if nothing else. There can be a feeling with the assistant that he could do as well as the head coach. This fact may be true, but it is easier for this feeling to manifest itself when ages are close — such as with a couple of young coaches in the same program — one the head coach, the other an assistant. This aspect will be covered when the "assistant coach" is reviewed.

Regardless of the situation, the head coach cannot delegate tough decisions, nor can he step aside and let others do some of the key coaching for him for any length of time. Some large situations are different, but everything there must be taught exactly as he wants it. The head coach cannot delegate too much, and he must be the one making key decisions. He must be the hardest worker, the one in control. Knowing what and how much to delegate is vital. Only time will allow the head coach to properly delegate. A guide to delegating decisions is to place yourself in the assistant's position. Treat the assistant as you would want to be treated. What your new assistant can best do may be a strong consideration in his role, as he may well be more limited in experience and with your personal philosophy. He could have a more direct focus due to lack of coaching experience. Perhaps a good beginning would be to utilize his strengths and at the same time teach him a new role so he may be soon educated to give you exactly what you need from the assistant position.

Another factor that adds to variation is that every situation is going to be different because of different personalities. Some head coaches are aloof, while their assistant complements them by being close to the athletes. This situation could be the other way around and still work. It could even be that they are of the same personality in relationship to the squad. Thus, one can readily see that there is a delicate blend, or marriage of purpose, that needs constant re-evaluation and reworking.

How many different kinds of relationships have you been exposed to?

Speculate why each relationship was like it was.

THE ASSISTANT COACH

The assistant coach may be a younger coach, learning and putting in an apprenticeship for his head job rather than going out on his own at this time, or he may be, as mentioned before, a well established assistant that does not want the worries of the head coach. He should have the same opportunities for respect and rewards from the same relationships as the head coach may have with the youngsters. I was once exposed to a great assistant coach who was in this latter category, and I am sure that he made a better assistant than a head coach. This assistant, in his particular role, could be "more himself." Perhaps his role was enhanced in this case because he did not have to deal quite the same as disciplinarian. A young assistant coach working up may often be thought of as the hardest worker, most loyal, etc., but not necessarily so. I am sure that there are many, many other combinations.

In any case, the assistant can be strong and have his own ideas, but what he teaches to the athlete must be in full agreement with the head coach. Time together is vital to this need. Loyalty to the direction set by the head coach is the key, or he has no place in the organization. If he cannot be loyal, because of whatever reason, then he must be loyal for that year and then leave. This does not mean that he cannot speak out to the head coach — in private. In fact, for both of them to learn from each other, they have to have a free exchange of ideas and a respect for each other's opinions, but once the issue has been batted around enough, they must be together on it when coaching the athletes. Both the head coach and the assistant should understand that their diversity can be a coaching strength, but what is taught must be the same. If disagreement in teaching occurs, you fail. The more diverse a staff or organization is, the more they must meet. The more the staff spends time together, the more they will genuinely agree with each other. The basic conduct, sacrifices, assets, and qualities must be pretty much the same for the assistant as for the head coach.

The assistant's rewards will also be much the same as that of the head coach. They have both labored and put their heart and soul in developing youngsters to be winners.

There is no question that experience does help the head coach. If you are an assistant, be understanding too, as only the experienced coach has lived through the problems of delegating too little or too much, the right things, and the wrong things. The older head coach has seen his role diminish and also has seen it enhanced by his dealings with his assistants. He has experienced assistants that have grown with him and made the organization much better and those that did not have a strong role. The relationship is the reward. As the head coach gets older, he grows in many ways, even though he may possibly experience some decline in coaching enthusiasm. *For sure, the one asset in which a head coach continually grows is in his working with his assistants.*

What should be the philosophy of a good assistant coach?

In your projected situation as an assistant, what is your ideal relationship?

THE MANAGER

The "most important person on a squad" is a good manager. The coach can delegate much responsibility to him and to other personnel that have committed to the program. This expands that which can be accomplished. The details are too numerous to mention. To delegate the right things makes the job of coaching much easier. If the coach has no manager or personnel to delegate duties related to organization, he is diminished greatly in his effectiveness. The season will be more difficult as the coach has to become a part-time manager.

Having gone through seasons where I had no help and others when there was adequate help, I appreciate the importance and place great emphasis on this position. Some administrators and coaches never learn to use other personnel for one reason or another. You can accomplish much more, be more productive, and do a better coaching job if you see things that need doing and find the proper way of delegating this responsibility. A good managerial system and related support system can allow the head coach to really grow. If a good system exists, the coach can delegate more each year.

Never allow your manager to bear the brunt of ridicule. Your young athletes are as cruel as they are nice. Be alert to the opportunities that come before the squad so that you can give your manager a top position within the group. He deserves recognition as much as the coach should appreciate his contribution.

Your manager is like any other youngster. He is seeking an identity and recognition by working for the squad. To deny this special place in the team's endeavors is like never recognizing an athlete for his contribution.

What can a coach do to enhance the managership role in his program?

THE VALUE OF MAINTENANCE

The dilapidation of a building, or an organization, is in progress when maintenance breaks down. This statement applies to nearly every phase of life. In coaching, if you do not keep things up, you are subject to decreased effectiveness when you least need it. It is like taking care of your car engine. Change the oil regularly, or soon you may have to change the engine.

The program that raises extra money and sets some aside for future needs, replaces equipment on a planned basis, takes pride in their facilities, has good account of everything spent, and still provides for improvement is practicing good maintenance. The coach is responsible for most of good maintenance practice. Be sure you appreciate this point, otherwise you are a "taker," not a "giver." Your program will reflect a down hill trend if you do not practice good maintenance. Your program will reflect positive growth if you practice good maintenance.

How do you rate the programs you are familiar with?

List other examples of good maintenance practices.

How can safety and even liability be enhanced by practicing good maintenance?

COACH-ATHLETE COMMUNICATION

Some coaches create their title and ask to be addressed in a certain way. They vision their role in a certain coach-athlete relationship. The beginning premise is how the athlete must speak to the coach. Could this infringe on the comfort zone of many athletes? Could this practice hamper communication? Yes. I have coached in systems where the athletes had to address the head coach by his last name, but as I look back, it did little to enhance feeling, respect, and consequently communication that led to their wanting to be led by him. If a title is your strength in gaining respect and discipline, then forget it. There is no argument that under some situations I could submit to this sort of formality, but I would not like being in it. The military is another issue.

It is not *what one says, but how one says it* that makes the big difference. If you have maximum communication, satisfy all athletes, and work toward the way to achieve by sharing, what does the name matter? Some athletes may want a special name (like your first name) just because it can't easily come out of them any other way. If it happens to be Coach (last name), so what? If it is his first name, then so what, too? If respect is there, there is no need to worry. If respect is not there, you need to worry, as titles will not help you. If they are not looking to you in losing contests or in other genuine ways, your title is hollow.

As a young athlete many years ago, I had a great coach at my high school. He had every credential, such as being a former Ivy League head coach prior to retiring to our small high school. Yet everyone that knew him called him by his first name. I named one of my sons after him. To have had to call him Coach (last name) would have seemed very much out of place. He was an intimate, feeling person, and we wanted to identify on that level. Incidentally, when this high school coach retired, past squad members gave him a car and a year's supply of gas. It seems that the in-tune way to look at it is that each coach is different — some are aloof, some are intimate, and some in-between. I have felt comfortable with some of the more aloof coaches I played for, calling them Coach (last name) or just Coach. To have had them force the issue of what to call them would have created a distance between some athletes and coach that need not be. Enough name calling — the topic is covered only because the approach varies greatly.

This topic is very debatable. What do you think is best for your situation?

What is most comfortable?

Should a coach ever be called by a nickname?

FRONT AND CENTER

A lot of people come to see contests, and the coach is constantly being judged. Fairly or unfairly, he is very often the one that is ultimately discussed. Classroom teachers can often turn in a poor effort and even produce a predominantly failing class(es) and survive. The coach sinks with his class if they are not successful. The competition could outclass him. The competition may also have been unfairly chosen. He is surfacely judged each time out by those looking only for a win, to vent their frustrations, or to just satisfy their egos by second guessing. Luckily, the final judgment usually comes from the word spread by the athletes and others "knowing" about the program. It is based rightly on how he teaches, how he relates, his example, etc.

In some situations, winning is overemphasized. It is sad to see some fine young coach have too much pressure on him. It can distort some of his values. If he is hired just to coach and if it is a pressure sport, he can become obsessed with his effort to the point of not tolerating a youngster's mistake. He can become a different person than he should be or wants to be. Personally, I would not like to place a classy youngster in such a situation and see him change or get unjustly hurt.

There are many roads to the top and all of them are related to the great variability of the "coach" and the "athlete." The coach has to be one of the best teachers in the system in order to pass the many tests. He is both fairly and unfairly judged. He is, nevertheless, on front and center stage.

How does the level you choose to coach affect the "Front and Center" emphasis?

A UNIQUE SITUATION

The coach succeeds because of many reasons. It is agreed he has a more advantageous position for teaching. Schools often have learning problems because they prepare youngsters for earning a living, or college entry, etc., and the teacher "dishes out" the material to be learned. The coach, however, can experience the joy of learning with youngsters that are *wanting* to learn. If they enjoy

the enthusiasm of learning in sport, they *may* want to tackle more
and varied things to learn. Why cannot learning in schools give the
youngster more in the line of fun learning — learning some of the
things he wants. Many students would catch fire and go far beyond
the achievement norm instead of being turned off to school. Failure
should not be so commonplace. It is a challenge for the classroom
teacher. A master teacher is resourceful and can appeal to the
student's natural motivations, whereas one can readily observe the
average teacher with *not enough of life's experiences and not resourceful enough to reach the student.* The average teacher wants
to be told the answers to teaching. There are none. The answer to
success lies in the teacher's own qualifications and commitment as
related to his *resourcefulness.*

In athletic endeavors, the teacher has an advantage. The athletic
curriculum is formulated around an intrinsic motivation of youth.
Thus, you cannot only teach them the sport they want to play but
you have their enthusiasm as a human venturing into life. The coach
can easily go beyond the classroom teacher. The youngsters, as
volunteers, are very often seeking excellence, and you have the information that can help them. There is no other place in the educational picture where the leader can actually demand excellence.
When you help a youngster, he grows, he feels good about himself,
and his interests surface. The classroom sees a lot of youngsters
just waiting for the bell to ring so that they can do something they
want to do. You, as coach, have a great audience looking to you.

There are other factors that those in administrative roles should
consider for better schools. *The traditional classroom offers
learning as a variable and time the constant.* In the classroom, the
length of class is constant. This means that in the classroom, the
student gets only so much done, depending on the time exposure.
Soon, class is over, and the student goes home to complete his assignment, which is oftentimes the same for everyone. The student
gets caught up or not; he may do quality work or put forth very
little substance. Then he returns to class for another assignment,
and soon the course is over. He receives his grade for what he
achieved. He may be average, and that is that. Learning is the variable. Contrast this traditional approach to what many medical
schools do. They do not want to turn out an "average" doctor.

Why? When you are sick, do you want to go to an "average" doctor? Therefore, they spend whatever time is necessary to accomplish a task — not a bare minimum sort of task as is often set forth as competence for completion of a unit, course, or graduation from high school or college. Being really good in an area gives one respect, confidence, and motivation. Mediocrity and mass production education could be eliminated. An individual could become outstanding and well known for his expertise in an area. Both the learner and the teacher would receive tremendous satisfaction.

The athlete and coach have it made. Their learning process builds confidence by achieving expertise that is pure in form and respected by all. The athlete's potential enthusiasm may be harnessed to tackle other areas. *The coach and the athlete work beyond the constant of time of the practice hours and even beyond the season to develop the youngster's physical and mental strengths.* Unique? Yes, and very important to the individual's growth and learning process.

There is another great plus within the uniqueness of the athlete's situation. If he becomes expert, beyond average, he elevates his whole pattern of attacking game problems. He goes beyond habit orientation with memory to allow his quick adjustment. He is now more apt to be an innovator. The person that has become excellent at something is skilled beyond the average and is more apt to invent ways to be even better. Perhaps intelligence and necessity are vital for invention, but for sure, the same motivation that moved the athlete from average to outstanding can help him invent a new technique to go a step further. Handling a basketball in the many new ways goes to the superior athlete, as he experimented on his own. He has gone beyond work that is habit and memory oriented. *To those who have achieved excellence in an area goes a much greater gift — experimentation and innovation.* Competition is greater in sport. The elations and depressions are greater. The factors of outstanding motivation, keen competition, and great elations and depressions provide a good learning situation for the athlete and for the coach. *Learning is the constant, time the variable.* Yes, unique.

Do you agree? Add your own thoughts to this perhaps controversial and certainly wide open topic.

THE COACH'S PERSONALITY

Individual personality seems to vary as much as any other human quality. It is easy to understand why there are so many different approaches to coaching. So what would you want for a coach's personality?

Some coaches might advocate that more control is gained out of fear than from a weaker posture. This type of coach would not express a real closeness. Others might naturally be very intimate.

Successful coaches are able to put things together with half a chance regardless of personality. However, if you enjoy talking to people, you are destined to have a lot more fun and rewards for your efforts. I envy the coach with a great sense of humor; the kids are especially close to him, and he is capable of harnessing this attachment and creating great morale. They'll have their share of wins for their situation. This seems to be the ideal.

Contrasted to a fun approach, the driving coach with little cheer, closeness, and perhaps even few compliments for work has created nearly a negative image. There is little one-to-one contact.

Can his rewards be as great? Is there greater power to win more often? Do the athletes like the day-to-day atmosphere? I doubt it. Personality combinations are numerous. You may not be the joking type. You may be intense but still one the athletes are close to. However, just appreciate the fun of youth, and along with your other assets, you are on your way.

The solely superorganized have their success. Some are just great recruiters. Others work harder on some details. Still others are great technicians and some great administrators. But the rewards and as many wins go to those really showing fun with each day.

You all have observed the griper, the uptight coach, the coach just waiting to be able to get at an official, the statistician, the excusemaker, the imagemaker, and those blaming the loss in irrelevant detail. How do you think others see you? Whatever your contributing strengths, I hope they see "joy."

How do you appraise your own personality?

What category would you create for you as coach?

How can the coach be a moderator for varying personalities on the squad?

SEEKING EXCELLENCE

Both coach and athlete are together by mutual interest. The athlete is a volunteer and is there to try to become as good as he can become.

I believe that most coaches would share the same opinion I have on the following statement: "There seems to be more all-around search for objectivity among athletes than among faculty." Sad, but true from where I looked at it. The athlete is innocent of politics, has a simple motivation, and is in a great setting for learning. Both the coach and the athletes are seeking excellence, not just the coach. It is an intense relationship that requires a lot from the coach. This is one of the reasons that the average coach's tenure is less than ten years. The coach has to stay on top of everything. The dedication required is the reason very few coaches go from beginning to retirement.

The striving for excellence is a very important aspect of all athletics, and nearly everyone that observes a top performance appreciates what the athlete has achieved. Spectators appreciate the work that went into the performance. *The athlete had to pass all tests, as his ability was frequently tested. There is no question left about the absolute achievement — it is known to all.* What was accomplished was not acquired in a business venture or by political means, but rather in open competition by fair rules. The achievement is unquestionable. One may not be able to make the same undeniable observations about the Presidency of the United States. This is why athletes are often chosen as widely acceptable hero identification symbols for advertising companies. The advertisers know that their product will be identified with someone successful that is respected by *all* because of given reasons.

The striving for excellence by the coach is a very real thing because he knows that the athlete is there by choice; he weighs his motivation factors and loads all he can towards complete dedication. This makes teaching easier and it makes the time spent most worthwhile. The end product is very satisfying for both coach and athlete.

Once again for emphasis — *there is no other setting in the formal educational picture where excellence can be demanded.* No average effort is accepted. No failure tolerated. Superb effort and achievement is the name of the game. Whatever effort necessary for success is expected and demanded by not only the coach but fellow athletes as well.

What other learning ventures approximate the striving for excellence found in athletics?

Can you evaluate the intensity?

DELEGATING

So that one may appreciate the need for delegation, here are a few of the jobs I listed that took my time in one sport I coached — some can be let go, others definitely not so. As full-time teacher and a college coach of swimming, these were things to do:

Spring (March 15) — follow up on acceptances of recruited athletes.

- letters
- calls
- visits
- meet with teammates to set next year's goals

April-May-June

- new letters recruiting
- inventory
- order equipment
- working on individual weaknesses

Summer
- letters to squad (3) personally written
- pool cleaned, equipment and facilities checked and in order
- record book, records filed
- summer recruiting

September – mid-February
- eligibility rules, forms, physicals
- 3 weeks: limited program, intramural swim
- water polo
- set up programs for individuals to follow
- some recruiting trips
- some campus visitations
- team meetings–rules, follow up on eligibility and physicals, dress, travel procedure, priorities, training room procedure, etc.
- meeting with captains
- swim-a-thon meetings, and active participation
- citrus sale, movies scheduled to create additional funding
- planning – managers and assistants geared for the season
- setting up details of fund raising
- pace "pick up" recruiting (listing priorities for admission)
- programs printed
- bulletin boards up-to-date
- planning for meets (some take 10-12 hours), planning practices (can take from 1/2 hour to 3 hours)
- scheduling officials for meets
- arrange bus or other transportation
- motel reservations
- trip itineraries
- postgame meal here for visitors or snack
- clean up
- meet results out next day
- remind maintenance of meet setup
- note sent to remind other team of meet time, ask if we can be of help, etc.
- scheduling videotape and seeing each athlete gets looked at 2 or 3 times
- scheduling pool for off hours for the year, i.e. Sundays, etc.

- be sure all meet equipment is available
- arrange for Florida trip
- cars to go, budgeting money for the southern trip
- Christmas notes reminding of total schedule for the third or fourth time
- always dealing with individual problems
- arrangements for meets on return southern trip
- more of the same, in concentrated season before the championship meet
- getting New Englands set up
    - events
    - drawing money
    - transportation
    - motel
    - issuing gas and meal money where necessary
    - getting entries in on time
    - getting list of swimmers in
    - seeing parents and recruiting at meet and along the way home
- recruiting acceptances, call to athletes (many disappointments, few elations)
- coming in mornings as in all of the year for early practices
- season ends with 3-day meet
- speaking at banquets and setting up our own (the cost, number, sending out invitations, getting votes for captain, and awards typed up)
- spring meetings, possibly nationals

Much of the work oftentimes cannot be delegated. Experienced managers and assistants can help a lot. When exhausted — be enthused. When things are going well — look for a real problem at the wrong time. When you're on top of "things to do" — you'll survive the daily crises. When you're even — it's potluck on how you will come out. When you are already behind — forget it, as sooner or later you will go under.

Consider your projected coaching needs and review your areas of delegation.

How many other areas can you add?

CHANGING PRIORITIES

As times change, the coach's job must change. Perhaps the most universal problem many sports face is a lack of adequate coverage in the media. With Title IX, the potential nearly doubled for media coverage. What good coverage some sports formerly enjoyed no longer exists. A problem was created. A sport is certainly relegated to low key without information reaching potential fans. The sports editors that used to cover your sport and write up the articles were unable to continue. Coaches became responsible for getting results and items of interest to the media in hopes of obtaining coverage. The changing priority was a distraction from actual coaching time. The coach may have to personally phone in results directly after a contest, and this is a particular time *when there are many other important duties to perform*. Many times this area can not be delegated.

As mentioned, fund raising is in focus for the teacher-coach. In order to meet your competition, you may be forced to spend additional time organizing and participating in the many kinds of fund raising. Your time is worth more than when you spend it on the details of raising funds — but is it? To survive, you must change priorities.

Off season commitments by the coach and athletes are also becoming more essential. Developing a feeder program by working with townspeople or coaching another team to get some of your athletes improving off season are definitely the coach's responsibilities.

A more affluent society with more financial independence and less discipline in social environment can be a factor in some situations and can change your priorities. Why? If a youngster has everything he wants, he oftentimes is less likely to be hungry when it comes to personal sacrifice and real physical and mental demand. If he has a pattern of social excess and lack of personal discipline, you have a problem some other coach may not have. There is often a vast difference between a boy brought up with hard labor and personal discipline and one used to the easy life with complete freedom.

Perhaps the above paragraph also denotes a changing emphasis for both coach and athlete. Physical conditioning has to be in greater focus due to social conditions in many communities. On the other hand, a more affluent society offers other kinds of opportunities for children. Perhaps skiing opportunities, tennis, golf, swimming, and summer coaching schools are just a few. At any rate, there are many factors at work to change the coach's priorities.

How many more can you list?

A COACH MAY NOT FIT

I once met a coach from a rural setting in the heart of a large city. He was not in his best element, just as a city being may not be as much at home in the most rural setting. He was there because he was winning a great percentage of his contests. This factor held him there. I questioned whether he was as effective as possible being in a situation that was not entirely compatible.

Sports and communities themselves are both quite variable too. A rough coach dealing with rough kids; it seems to work. The more feeling coach may find a lot of hurts from critics and problems he does not expect from the athletes. He can still be successful and get the things he wants done, but it takes longer and he will always have some regression. He is in a foreign environment. Even though basically youngsters are all much the same, they differ from sport to sport and from community to community.

I found great satisfaction in coaching the internal football lineman, and I found it especially easy to relate to youngsters at a small midwestern college. However, as I experienced new situations, there were tremendous satisfactions in dealing with another kind of youngster, a different kind of sport, and from athletes of a very different background — namely, swimmers. The point made is that a sensitive coach in some situations could be years longer accomplishing his discipline at a much greater price to himself.

Some sports have physically tough athletes and they reflect this. Other athletes enjoy noncontact endeavors and they, too, reflect this. There are many other variables of this nature that bear on the relationship of coach and athlete. A good coach can make it anywhere, but to utilize the economy of your time and talents and enjoy coaching to the fullest, it is enhanced by the right situations for you. Changing positions when you are young can give the coach a way of evaluating this aspect.

Have you experienced good coaches that could have been more effective if coaching in a different situation?

What kind of other situations have you experienced?

Have you experienced coaches in clashes with differences in administrative philosophy?

REFLECTIONS: THE WAY OF A COACH

Having fun playing. Liking people. Gaining inspiration from good coaches.

Wanting to teach and educate through sport. Preparing in many ways.

Committing yourself to the season. Taking on the related commitments.

Dealing with faculty. Making up and giving tests. Grading papers. Evaluating and being evaluated.

Trying to catch up on mail. Preparing on the run. The never ending recruiting. Giving tours.

Financing your program. Selling. Budgeting.

Updating the bulletin board. Dealing with your superiors. Asking for what you need. Getting shot down regularly but never becoming gun shy. Being loyal when it's hard.

Always keeping your professional attitude and creating enthusiasm everywhere.

Lots of meetings. Many unimportant.

Making time to answer questions. Making time for untimely problems.

Sometimes issuing equipment, then collecting same. Keeping your many records straight.

Long hours. Never getting done. Not forgetting to arrange for physicals. More rosters to be run off. Organizing, distributing, and storing players handbooks.

Illustrating great patience. Sometimes reprimanding. Always quick to forgive.

Short notice deadlines. Justifying your programs.

Lining fields. Setting up. Taking down. Delegating responsibility so you can do more for the program.

Remembering details that make for winnings. Forgetting details that don't help the situation.

Mindful of public relations. More awards lists. Banquets and honoring the work of athletes. Booster clubs and service clubs. Coaching in the summer recreation program.

Hungry athletes and happy kids. Kids that make your day. Then kids too much to want anything. One or two that make your season especially enjoyable. Always one to two that never let the ideal squad take shape.

Living around locker room smell. Working out regularly and getting things off your mind. Showering. Dressing and undressing many times a day. Keeping locker rooms under control. Perhaps a moment of lack of control.

An expert at first aid. Going to emergency rooms. Notifying parents. Surely making time to visit. Much time in the training room. Running on the field to start practice. Concentrated life for certain.

Long bus trips. Changing players attitudes. Returning home late. Some cars don't start. Extra hours of taking kids home. Too many late nights.

Whistles. Fouls. Controlling your emotions. Expressing great emotion. Good breaks. Bad breads. Good refs. Some not so good.

Losses. Some easier to take. Others never shaken off. Perhaps being outcoached and never forgetting it. Unreasonable fans. Dealing with parents. Being your own consoler. Real lows.

Harnessing people power. Workmanship wins. Some great wins. Elations like no other. Chills up your spine. Being carried off the field. Your efforts all seem worthwhile.

Persisting. Trying to peak and taper right. Learning how to better isolate and teach all kinds of fundamentals. Giving yourself rewards when you do well. Taking them away when you don't do so well.

Learning from everyone and everything that happens. Becoming an expert game administrator. Knowing how to win with half a chance. Maturing fast with every season. The feeling that you are master at what you do. Running scared so you will keep feeling that way.

You have teams with great character. Teams that had little. Many just plain characters. Winning enough to make them believers. Things get harder. Rewards are greater. You continue to see and enjoy each one another time around.

Wearing out but not showing a loss of zip. Never rusting out. Needing more time to heal. Just a little rest and you're back for more the next day. A little more rest and you're back again next year. Looking back with great memories and much satisfaction. How did it go by so fast? I would not want my life to go any other way.

Sound familiar? Add or subtract to fit your experiences.

Chapter 3

SOME BASICS

ORGANIZATION

BEING "underorganized" is a problem. Overorganization can also be a problem. Let's say that being well organized is vital to success. It takes care of many of the surprise problems of the unorganized coach. It is devastating to all when an unforseen problem arises and there is no real time to deal with it. If the coach is prepared, he has fewer surprises, the team reflects his high degree of motivation, and they are more apt to have good mental preparation and morale. Good organization also is directly related to the athlete's physical condition. The poorly organized coach, for sure, is in for surprises. He has more discipline problems. His athletes are working at less than their best. They do not have great morale.

There is a limit to organization. It can cut into flexibility, personal contact, and even morale. But be sure you consider all the vital areas before your season. Be sure you prepare well for each day of the season. A special emphasis will be given on orientation, but the purpose of organization is to achieve better orientation for the athlete and even to gain his *help*.

How does organization in this context relate to business, armed forces, handling any group, or other lines of endeavor?

FLEXIBILITY AND PATIENCE

Just as being flexible can gain rapport and more achievement for the coach, so does an extra bit of patience. Setbacks in attaining your goals are just a "fact of life." The coach has to realize that in some situations, his goals, philosophy, and other important components can be achieved fairly rapidly, while *in other situations,* things can be very, very slow. Perhaps the coach has to give some, perhaps even change some, if he is to accomplish the greatest good. It is difficult to emphasize the point of the coach having to make major adjustments. However, if the adjustments are sound and within his broad philosophy, there can be great dividends. It is a more compatible situation when the coach can be flexible.

It is often not a compatible situation when everyone has to fit his mold. Not every situation is blessed to fit the coach. Coaches that have moved a few times must appreciate this point. In fact, just about all situations would be less than ideal. The trick is to not let the situation destroy any of your talent. You may not control it entirely, but never let it control you. *Give,* but keep your self-respect and your basic coaching philosophy. Harmony is sought but not at all cost. Don't forget that it is possible for major conflicts between athlete and coach to end up in the closest of associations. *Your job is not to lose good people unnecessarily but rather to harness their talent and make them gain confidence in their abilities. If you can't give any more of yourself and still keep your self-respect, forget it.* A great coach and great athlete *may not make it together. This is the ultimate challenge.*

The athlete is a human being and as such has had past experiences. Some experiences have been to bolster his confidence and others have been to the contrary. The success-failure pattern may play an important role in how he will normally react to defeat. There seems to be a direct proportional relationship. The failures, if great in number, may well mean that he cannot take in normal fashion the defeats that most athletes can deal with. Confidence and steadiness go with success. The flexible and patient coach has to mesh his goals with the athlete's talent as he finds it. The sensitive coach understands the differences in athletes. Other coaches the athlete has had in the past, different family experiences, varying expectation levels, and physical capacities are other variables that challenge a coach's flexibility and patience. The coach's experience can add greatly to his appreciation of the terms "flexibility" and "patience."

Cite situations where flexibility and patience is needed. Cite situations where it is not a part of the coach's role.

THE RIGHT ATTITUDE ABOUT YOUR PROGRAM

For a coach to be myopic is understandable. However, it is common to observe coaches taking themselves and what they do too seriously. Some programs have been overemphasized. Overemphasis of a program can even contribute to other program deemphasis. Overemphasis also has been a strong contributing factor in why some programs have been dropped. The coach as well as the athletic director has a responsibility here.

Coaching was referred to as a "young man's" game. Overwork is common and, as mentioned, can lead to early retirement. It is very difficult for one to gear one's efforts for the long haul. The pressure is there to work every minute. Some coaches I have known have done just that — myself included for long periods of time. However, if the person is a normal human being and likes some other things, all work and no play gets old after a few years. *Know what the program should be in your situation — it is healthy for the sport itself.* Also be aware of the too much work ethic and your leaving coaching early. It is sad to *frequently* observe potentially outstanding coaches work so hard for the rewards that they leave coaching.

If a coach thoroughly enjoys what he is doing, it permeates others and gives a proper atmosphere for productive and positive effort. If the coach is overly serious, he influences others in this way. If he is obsessed with himself and with winning, there often is little fun for anyone involved. This is not what it is all about.

In some sports, the coach just has to love the kids. With no publicity, little school emphasis, poor facilities or budgets, and little following, what else can be the atmosphere? It is just as productive as being too serious. Just do your best, the coach should be demanding of this at all times. Then, if the results are not on the positive side of the ledger, the coach has to be understanding and convey this. If the athlete is dedicated to doing his best, the results take care of themselves over the long haul. Hear the right vibes. Don't take yourself or your working life too seriously.

Record the different situations you have observed where the coach actually was less effective because of being too serious.

PUTTING THINGS TOGETHER

The season starts with a dream of a great year. You start with a positive approach to high goals. What are other factors that greatly affect putting things together? Leadership from the squad is one aspect that is ever changing. What happens in any one year, from either the coach's output or that of the athlete, is *only* for that year. This fact is just like the game to game change of attitude. Oftentimes a winning, or outstanding, team will have all of the athletes coming back and it will seem just like a fact of life that another great season will take place. So many would-be great teams have slipped into mediocrity as the season progresses. The competition is different, and the running scared, but confident, attitude may be lacking. After you have a Thanksgiving dinner, you are not hungry. Neither is a team apt to be quite so "hungry" after winning all of the honors. It is commonplace for seemingly championship senior and even junior teams to be dethroned. The young team, often lacking in experience, can often be your greatest satisfaction. What the coach did was to take potential, make them believe, and watch it happen. Perhaps the vitality of any organization is resting with the younger, more enthusiastic, and often harder working members. At any rate, coaching experience will help set the right attitude. The great coach can better sort out this phenomenon and combine other components, as he has learned more about what it takes to win. "Knowing how to win" seems like an odd statement. However, some coaches do a topflight job, but just don't seem to get it all together. These coaches in essence do not know how to win.

Aside from keeping a squad running confident but worried, a winning coach is always coming up with a special analysis of *his* talent, special offenses or defenses to be more efficient. This coach is innovative, uses the strengths in his athletes, and knows how to win.

Third, and this relates to the first aspect, constant awareness of day-to-day and week-to-week happenings is vital. This coach can better give them the winning key at the right time. To orient athletes to every changing situation is the key. The coach who knows how to win is always working on finding the "key" to create a focus for the squad for that week.

Some people are natural winners from early childhood. In almost any game, they know how to win — others are slower to learn how to put things together, and still others just don't ever put it all together. Years of playing and coaching may especially help the middle category. Years of experience may have little effect on the latter category. There is no guarantee for success.

Just as the outstanding football running back probably gains most of his cutting ability and finesse from countless hours of backyard play, the inexperienced coach can greatly enhance his "putting together" ability by coaching more than one sport in a year. To coach an eight game football season means you only had eight chances to put things together to win in that year, but to coach another fifteen game season, perhaps with basketball, greatly improves the potential to learn how to win. One may not be able to coach two or three sports a year much of his life — especially on the more competitive levels. However, it is great experience for the young coach — like two years in one.

How many coaches do you know who really put things together?

How many do you know who do a fine job but lack the winning edge?

A GREAT AID

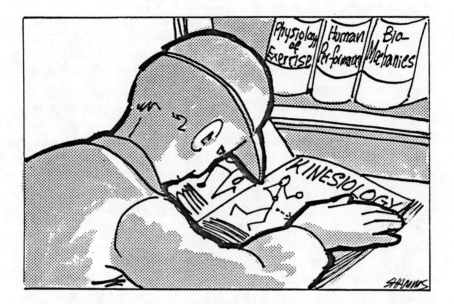

Let's assume the coach establishes proper goals, works hard, is updated in his knowledge of his sport, and is a great game technician. The day-to-day application of scientific principles should always be a foundation of practice organization and of the teaching of techniques.

Whatever is taught should be done because it is vital to the athlete to perform better. What is taught should be very *selective and necessary* — this cannot be assumed. The knowledge of kinesiology (the study of body movement) and physiology of exercise should underlie much of what is done. A coach with a very complementary knowledge of how the body most efficiently moves according to scientific principles is at a definite advantage over one that is teaching a technique the way he has had it taught to him. The truly professional coach knows the "why" of his teachings. Sounds unusual? No. Many coaches teach without knowing exactly what is needed. Many more coaches teach without knowing what is mechanically correct.

Physiology (the study of body function) should also govern such things as what kinds of workouts are needed — repetition, interval, and emphasis on muscular strength and endurance are just a few considerations. The balance in practice sessions of stress and rest, nutritional needs, peaking, and tapering are just a few of other physiological considerations. The exact balance must be incorporated into practice to make it not only interesting but exactly what each athlete needs. To train track men for sprints, distance, or field events, one can easily see that the workouts have to be individual. In other sports, different team sports, where more numbers are involved, to have the practice meet each individual's needs is better done from a sound background in physiology.

Take a look at John Bunn's book on *Scientific Principles of Coaching* or another text in this vein, and you will see how mechanical analysis of body movement aids the teaching of technique. The aforementioned applied with a kinesiological muscular analysis of the skills involved makes for the professionally oriented coach. To coach without a knowledge of physiology, kinesiology, specifically needed mechanical principles, and first aid is like a mechanic working on your car who has never taken an engine apart to see how it worked, but rather replaces parts until he finds the trouble. Coaching is a race against time, especially during a season, and it is vital to do things right the first time. Furthermore, *the coach is working with human beings,* and valuable time cannot be given by the athlete for trial and error approaches. The safety of athletes is constantly linked to good use of these sciences. Surprisingly, parents and athletes often tolerate coaching errors of this nature, but they will not tolerate a mechanic that is replacing parts as a trial error approach to their car problem. The coach owes it to himself and to those he teaches to make every preparation in these basic bodies of knowledge. It can offer a lot of answers to everyday questions. The outstanding coach will very often first consider the principles of body movement and function in arranging any practice.

Can you recall coaches with good biomechanical backgrounds who were better teachers of their sport because of this specialized kind of knowledge?

PROBLEMS ASSOCIATED WITH COACHING

Often, facilities, finances, and the administration deal with the direct success of a program. It is commonplace for the "defeated" coach to criticize these shortcomings. However, more often than not a coach fails from his own common shortcomings.

If he fails to teach and prepare his teams adequately and they perform in a slipshod manner, he will be in for much criticism. What he teaches shows.

If he fails to have community support due to his life-style or relationships with townspeople, he is in for problems.

If he fails to deal squarely with his athletes and/or does not promote good team morale, it will filter down to those in the community. He may lose this key support. The best public relations will come forth by the way athletes speak about him and the program to parents and community members.

If he does not condition his athletes properly, he has many related and different problems.

If he does not work exceptionally hard at what he does, he will reap the loafing and undisciplined athletes in contests. If he has a problem here — it's "gonzo."

If he has a personal conflict with his superiors, he may also be in for big trouble, as very few individuals are "big" enough to be able to forget an exchange of harsh words. Most of the time, he is doomed for the short end and might as well stay very loyal until his responsibilities end and then leave.

The coach can be quite limited. Lack of talent causes concern. The coach cannot make chicken salad from chicken feathers. The program may just have a schedule that does not allow for winning. Maybe a specific coach should not have taken over that particular challenge.

Good coaches prepare extremely well during the week and greatly enhance winning that way. Other coaches may not be as well organized but can win by being excellent technicians and game administrators. If you don't have both assets, you had better have one or the other just to survive.

The coach's emotional approach can also add or detract depending on his control.

Some coaching positions are pressure situations — the coach must win to be able to stay. Again, maybe he should have thought twice before accepting the position. This situation can challenge your value judgments, and thus problems occur.

Other communities do not care about your sport, and this is a big negative.

On and on to the minutia of lacking experience, thus listening too much to strong players or outside advice.

Even the weather can be a hindrance to your sport. Problems you didn't have to have. A baseball coach in the north country is hard put to accomplish what his colleague can in the sunny south.

If the reader is interested in problems limiting a coach's ability to analyze, refer to Andrew Grieve's article in *Athletic Journal*, volume 51, June 1971, pp. 42-45 and 53-54.

YOUR JOB

It often takes a few years before one has the strength of conviction not just to teach what he had been taught. This factor has been stressed. When the coach relies on his knowledge of scientific principles to reason out his teachings, he is becoming engulfed in his own strengths. When you can look at an athlete and give a ten minute dissertation on what he can do exceptionally well, or not well, you know him and what he can do best for the team. This is your job. As emphasized, the study of kinesiology is a great aid in developing this independent and sound judgment. But in whatever case, *you have to harness each individual strength and hide the weaknesses* if you are to use the potential power you have out for the squad. What a waste to take a Kentucky Derby winner and try to win a pulling contest with him. You should not fit the system to the athlete but rather emphasize what can be done by your best athletes and find a system best suited for them. A coach that does not have a handle on everyone's strengths is not a coach. His job is to bring out the best in each athlete and in each team. To do less than this is placing your athletes and team in competition with a "stacked deck" against them. Only time will allow the coach to become more articulate in scouting out coordination, agility, speed, muscular strength, flexibility, muscular endurance, cardio-respiratory appraisal, balance, mental attitude, competitive spirit, dependability, the injury free and injury prone, the blue chipper, and those having trouble in tight situations. Knowing what qualities your athletes have, the qualities you need to enhance, and which athletes will profit most by your efforts helps you develop each athlete and place him properly as a team member. This is *Key*. Read Don Veller's "Get the Right Boy in the Right Job," *Athletic Journal,* volume 46, March 1966, pp. 46-54 and 85-87 for some examples and factors in placing personnel. Talking with some older coaches and asking how they made mistakes as well as how they did well in placing personnel will benefit any young coach.

Observe your team and scout out your strengths and weaknesses, and set forth better ways to emphasize strengths and hide weaknesses.

ANOTHER THING YOU LEARN

The experienced coach knows that over the years he may, if in an even competitive situation, be on the short end as many times as on the winning side, and he must always be sensitive to those not so fortunate that afternoon. To be known as a gentleman and a competitor is a most honorable goal — it's what it is all about. There can be no room to harbor hate from past contests. To seek revenge fosters hate. Remember this — if you do something for sport that is not good such as beating a team 50-0 when there is an acceptable way to prevent it, you are then hurting youngsters, it is not good for the sport, and you are hurting yourself. Neither team really benefits if the coach is not alert to the good teaching opportunities in this kind of situation. If you have ever been in a locker room with the short end of the final score being tremendously uneven, you know what I am talking about. Sometimes an inexperienced coach can find little to say to his losing group, and in some contact sport situations, the athletes could really be set back for the season.

You as a coach must foster the above principles or they will not come out and happen in the athletes' exposure. To a great extent, the athletes "mirror" your teachings. Just as you can walk into a high school when classes are changing and tell quite a bit about discipline, so can another coach tell a lot about his colleagues by how that coach's athletes act. Not always true? Right. But behind any poorly acting team you will probably find a poor example by the coach. Even more supporting, genuine show of sportsmanship and class in tough situations reflects directly on the coach and what he has taught them.

Review situations where coaches have been poor examples and good examples.

Ever see any good come from a contest where one-sided scoring was out of control?

What are some ethical approaches to keep an uneven contest in check? Explain your attitude about next year's contest after your team lost by a much larger margin than you felt was necessary.

CHANGING VALUES

Being as close as sport teams are, there is often the chance to become quite intimate in conversation. It is common for a youngster to seek your opinion or advice on matters so intimate that no other person would be considered a confidant. You are often in the center of an important phase of an individual's development.

One of the key settings is on the bus. The argument for taking busses is a safety one, but the bus also offers a closeness. The privacy and space relationships offer a verbal exchange often lacking in many other settings. For example, locker rooms are oftentimes not private. When you speak to your squad pregame, when their interest is high, then you have used the "golden moment" because you at least had the bus for your group. After the contest, the bus is often the best place to sum up your afternoon's efforts; it is the most teachable moment. This moment must be capitalized upon. When cars or vans are used, the teachable moment is often not there. Being confined focuses on what you want as an atmosphere after contests. After a while, the game may be forgotten and the young minds go to their intimate questions.

Some travel situations, I am sure, promote poor language and poor conduct, while others foster the best in behavior and the best in building values. I remember the personal talks on the trips as a highlight of my coaching career.

There are other settings that offer a prime chance — preseason training camps, the locker rooms, the gathering place such as your office, at your home, or at relaxed individual meetings. Values become a part of most everything discussed.

What values are most commonly enhanced?

What situations were you exposed to that offered a special coach-athlete exchange?

What other situations can the coach create to foster closeness?

DAY-TO-DAY ACCOMPLISHMENTS

Excellent practices where everyone has a super day and everything is done just right do not seem to come every day. It can save you grief if you realize that you don't have everything your way all the time. You can count on one hand the number of times you find three excellent practices occurring in a row during the season. Two outstanding practices are common. This is why coaches often organize their practices so that they demand a hard day, then alter practice, and then return to the hard day again. Whether your pattern for the week is hard-hard-easy or hard-easy-hard, there is much that can be accomplished in a relaxed atmosphere. Being prepared to expect reality is important to your own personal long term satisfaction. It is also important for the athlete to realize the achievements each day cannot all be alike. Letting squads go early if they do something well is an example of how a coach might adjust to an average or poor day. He realizes that it just is not in the cards to have a productive day. If you can salvage some good morale, you have adjusted and may even be able to control the next day much better after the extra rest they will have. Stress and rest is what makes for development, and to harness this idea in daily practices for optimum results is an art you will do better with each year you coach. No one can outline the right program for you and your group, and only your "feel" from experience can get the maximum benefits. Do not misinterpret — the athlete's super concentration as he approaches practice will most generally be quite apart from the coach's expectations.

How many coaching situations have you been associated with where the stress-rest syndrome was not considered by the coach?

How can you help your athletes mentally do their best each day by adhering to the cycles of hard work?

TWO THINGS THAT MAKE A COACH HAPPY

One of the elations a coach gets for his constant efforts comes at the conclusion of practice. It's a great feeling to know that your athletes worked especially hard that afternoon. It makes the day worthwhile. In contrast, to feel that things went poorly or that the athletes did not give their best is like putting in lots of time for nothing. Without this feeling of knowing the athletes worked hard, you cannot be happy. The athletes cannot be happy either.

The other thing that made the day for me was to see hard work along with a happy athlete. *Happiness and enthusiasm, along with great effort, is the duo that makes the coach happy.* It makes him feel that this is the best thing he could be doing with his time. You also feed your soul on youth's enthusiasm. It keeps you young. To observe a youngster putting out his maximum and coming up for more with an enthusiastic smile is more reward than some people get from their work in years. To see an athlete really achieve his goals and to see continued success in later life are other things a coach needs.

What are additional happenings that you would like to experience to make you happy?

COACHING YOUR OWN CHILDREN

Many coaches, sooner or later, have to face the problem of whether to coach their own children or whether it is better to have their children play for another coach.

The first argument is a justification. You are good at your field. You know that each coach is different and you want *your own* philosophy passed on to your son or daughter. It is tremendously satisfying to see your own children grow under your guidance. You are also in the best position to know all there is to know about your offspring and therefore do a better job of bringing them along.

You also spend a lot of your life away from your family, and this may be your best way to have some concrete athletic experience with your children. Remember, many coaches neglect their own families because of time demands. Possibly you may only have the chance to coach them while they are in their earlier years. Then they go on, and you may not ever even see them play as you are tied up on game days with your own team. Thus, you eagerly go forward into the venture with your children.

An argument for not coaching your own children is that they may not as readily accept what you say. It often is easier for them to turn off their father than to not respond to a coach from outside the family. Another coach may hold a different position in your youngster's life. Your youngster is not constantly with the outside coach at home and other hours. Your child may have a more natural coach-athlete relationship.

Another negative for the father-son situation is that the coach, in trying to be fair, may be more demanding on his own child. If the child senses his father being extra hard on him or interprets his father's actions as not of a coach, this can create a breach between coach (father) and athlete (son).

The coach, as father, is also around his children on an intimate basis and often brings *too much teaching* into the family relationship. It is difficult to forget coaching your children when not at practice. Thus, undue pressure can be created for the youngsters.

Another negative is that personal prejudices often can creep in and you may believe more in *your own child's potential,* as any normal parent may. The coach's youngster could be in a situation where he is given a position on the team that is open for question by others. This is a tough situation in which to place your youngster.

There is another reason for not coaching your own. It is possible your child will be able to compare his outside coach to your way and learn from a wider exposure. Perhaps he would come to really appreciate your approach.

So, what do you do? It is certainly a personal choice. It is a choice that has many facets. My personal experience was that I was away from my own so much that when I had the chance to coach them, I wanted to be with them. I could combine work time and family time, so to speak. Second, even though they might not listen quite as closely as they would to an outside-of-the-family coach, they did believe in your knowledge. You had your youngster's respect and he had a normal experience. I felt that I knew their abilities and would deal fairly with this. If my youngsters were qualified, they played a certain position, and if they were not, they knew it, and then they knew why. This factor is a key one and one that must be answered early by the parent coach. It is certainly even more complicated if two of your children want the same position. It happened to me, and I almost wish I had opted for letting someone else coach them. However, the greatest of satisfactions comes to you, as coach-father, when you bring out your own child's strengths, and he develops ability and confidence before your eyes.

If you feel you can be objective and not be easier or tougher on your youngster, *then do it*. If you have reservations, then it may be preferable to have an outsider coach your children. This appears to be a simple clear-cut way of deciding what to do, but each factor has to be weighed differently in each family, as each coach and child are different. Thus, there is a multifaceted decision to be made. It would be the ideal for me to see every coach feel totally objective and comfortable with the decision to work with his own children and have his youngster as well as his teammates feel the same way.

How do you feel at this point in time?

Chapter 4

RELATIONSHIP VALUES AFFECTING YOUR JOB

THE COACH HOLDS A SUPER POSITION

W̶E have made the case for the coach being in the best position in the educational picture to enhance an individual's values and help youngsters live better lives. The coach's job is much easier when the program is philosophically supported by the administration. If the administration also supports the program financially and if the program has goals that are compatible with the school's philosophy, the setting for good growth exists.

To what goals can the coach and the top administrator of the school subscribe? Other than trade schools or commercial schools, most institutions support the *goals* of general education. The idea is to develop a more effective citizen, not just a person that is measured "successful" by his preparation to make a living, to earn money, or an individual seeking the truth. Your goal is *to develop a total individual that is a contributing member of his society.*

Individual courses in the school's system often deal more with the specific educational objectives. Athletics offers tremendous *all-around* contributions to the objectives of general education. To catch the idea of a few common attainments, the following paragraph refers to one of the most obvious objectives — "self-realization."

The objective of "self-realization" can be met very easily in sport and through the team atmosphere. Good health habits, fitness, responsible direction to life, and recreational background for later life are stated subobjectives. The respect for human relations through lasting friendships, getting along with people, cooperating, being a leader or good follower, courtesy, respect for others, etc., are natural to sport and are also subobjectives of "self-realization." There are many, many other values that are easily identified in athletics. Each subject and extracurricular pursuit has its special opportunity to contribute, but there is no field quite so fertile for channeling a youngster's enthusiasm to meet the objectives of education. When I have listened to the goals of some educators of only advancing truths at perhaps the cost of producing hate and counterproductive efforts, it makes me feel that coaching has tremendous depth. Why not combine this with a basic value expressed by Abraham Lincoln. "A man should live his life so that he is proud of his community and his community is proud of him." The demonstrations in our country have not been chartered by our athletes, nor have they often been conducted with the above premise in mind. Athletes have been too busy harnessing positive thoughts, channeling enthusiasm, and developing physical talent through sport. I am not advocating that groups should not speak out for right causes; in fact, that *is a responsibility*. However, the coach likes spending his time harnessing the innate enthusiasm to the enjoyable pursuit at hand. I believe that working in the "positive" begets positive results. It is a great way to develop responsible and positive citizenship. The coach truly has a super position for the opportunity of harnessing positive things for a better place in which to live. Positive approaches are always better than approaches that are negative.

What is the aim of general education?

What are the objectives?

Review all of the objectives of general education and relate how sport can be the greatest contributor to the academic goals of general education.

Defend the sport of your interest as a contributor to the objectives of education.

A SPECIAL ASPECT OF ATHLETES

The "physical prowess drive" that youngsters have is a natural way of recognition. The coach has to capitalize on the youngster's need to excel physically in order to create the best avenue for psychological adjustment.

When a youngster uses his natural physical vigor and enthusiasm and gains recognition from it, great things can happen. He wants recognition. Physical accomplishment is a natural way. When this does not happen, all sorts of other manifestations can surface, for example, a youngster's behavior can go from quiet assurance when he is successful to boisterousness, stemming from insecurity caused by lack of physical status. The coach should be aware for the need for physical status and best use the physical assets of the athlete. Avenues become available to develop an individual's mental assets as well. Relate the physical success that is carefully planned to positive value attainment.

How often have you observed a youngster in athletics who is highly motivated through his physical prowess drive?

How can you capitalize on this need with the very young athlete? With the high school athlete?

CONCENTRATED LIFE

Hour for hour, there is nothing in the educational picture that can mature both the athlete and coach as much as their going through a sport season from start to finish.

The person that has everything "squared away" all of the time in life is without its pitfalls and will not experience what is necessary for the maturing process. If life is just a "bowl of cherries" or an even line, something is missing. This is never the case in a sports season. Maturation requires effort, chances, pitfalls, and not just time. The coach also learns by concentrated life. If he has the chance to coach two sports, he is getting double the opportunity to mature. The golden moments of the games, practices, and experiences are all doubled. As previously stressed, learning about people and ways to better lead is greatly enhanced by multiple coaching assignments.

When athletes come to you with their minicrises, it always is at an inappropriate time, and yet the athlete has to have your understanding and involvement. This is life in concentration.

Another example of concentrated life that really hits home is a phenomenon that happens to all who participate in the season. There are no other experiences in the school's curriculum that allow the participant to get to know so many other people as well in such a given, limited period of time. This means they experience joy and sadness together. They are tired and have troubled times, even abrasive experiences. There are great elations from great team effort and great pitfalls. There is both idle and intense time together. They get to know each other, not just as a teammate but as a person with special qualities and interests. They do not forget each other in their lifetime. That's concentration.

How can the coach capitalize on the concentrated life aspect of sport?

THE ACADEMIC SETTING

Rhetoric alludes to the search for truth. Many professors would seem to feel that they have a corner on objectivity. However, many of these same advocates are very narrow in their definition of exactly what education for the youngsters is all about. "I regard it as the foremost task of education to ensure the survival of these qualities: an enterprising curiosity, an undefeatable spirit, tenacity in pursuit, readiness for sensible self-denial, and above all compassion" (Kurt Hahn, source unknown). This is an example of a broad definition. I find it acceptable. However, *many of the teaching faculty do not understand and appreciate the many facets to educate youth.* This is disheartening and something an intelligent coach just has to often live with. Sorry to have to say it.

The lack of objectivity is often encountered when various departments and faculty personnel are trying to gain an advantage to themselves. Politics always seems to be a part of the educational picture. Sorry again. In athletics, there is no maneuvering, no doing a fellow in for selfish gain. There is very little chance for politics among athletes or among coach and athlete. Everyone is on an equal basis. As emphasized before, what is achieved is pure achievement and recognized by all as such. To observe an athlete analyzing a game film after practice or to watch him seek every avenue to learn all he can about a technique is observing objectivity in purest form. The coach has fantastic opportunities to teach and educate youngsters in many ways. His unique vehicle is large muscle activity that he carefully maneuvers as to kind and outcome.

What are some common relationships of athletics to the academic setting? A coach may check on the progress of an athlete in all good faith, but may appear to be putting pressure on a faculty member for a student's grade. This kind of happening can be a detriment to the athletic image; some faculty are a bit touchy and feel that any direct questions are a form of pressure. I have witnessed a teacher becoming very aggressive when a coach checked on one of his athletes. The coach sees his athletes every day and is in a position to help them back on the right track. However, the teacher may feel he is being pressured. Perhaps the above example was just a misunderstanding, but that teacher may always harbor a negative reaction about athletics due to a coach checking — perhaps beyond that instructor's bounds. It hurts all concerned; be extra careful of your dealings with teachers about the progress of your athletes. Many teachers like you and I would welcome inter-

est from a coach because of his closeness with the athlete. Others
see this as pressure. In the pressure situation, there is often undue
pressure to win, and coaches with shaky values have sought grade
changes or have changed transcripts to afford eligibility. This kind
of happening creates the worst possible athletic image. Pressure
situations can bring out the worst at the coaching level, *but it is
especially sad when university presidents are aware and are really
part of unethical acts.* This is the saddest of all happenings. The
administrators are the ones setting the policy, and they really are
the ones sanctioning or creating this sort of thing. If they do not
know what is happening, they should be held accountable for
gross neglect.

Another relationship of athletics to the academic atmosphere
is when athletes have to miss class to attend a contest. Especially
is this a negative when the athlete fails to see the teacher ahead of
time, fails to present himself properly, or fails to make up the
work. Sometimes schools have an excuse policy whereby the
athlete brings a signed slip to the teacher to indicate he is excused.
Whatever the official excuse, it is finally the way in which the
youngster approaches the teacher that makes the difference. If
the teacher will not cooperate, the youngster should stay behind
for class or take the test, etc. Then, at a later date, this problem
can be discussed in the proper atmosphere. A lot of problems do
arise from lack of communication between the athlete and teacher
prior to missing a class. It is the coach's responsibility to completely orient his athletes so that they will have the proper attitude
in class. It is true that some teachers will never change a prejudiced
attitude, and that is their right. If they believe in the youngster's
endeavors, then they do. If they do not believe in the total education of the individual, then they do not. If they don't know where
it is at, then it is their problem, not ours, even though their im-
mature attitude hurts all concerned.

A plus for the relationship is for the coach to be a conscien-
tious faculty member. The professional person balances his enthusiasm for coaching, demands that are nearly consuming him, with
the activity and academic class assignments. Those who have
balance deserve a particular respect. They will also get more
support for their program. The point made here is that the aca-

demic setting is not perfect and does have a great influence on many aspects of coaching.

Recall the situations you have observed where the athletes have been hurt by narrow-thinking faculty. Also recall with equal emphasis the ways in which the "real teachers" have shown their understanding of what "education" is all about.

BREAKING DOWN PREJUDICES

Coaches and physical education teachers are often viewed apart from the regular faculty. Some of the blame must go to the coach who does not attend meetings, does not spend time with other faculty, does not dress his best for his many roles, or does not appreciate his total faculty role. Even though he is subject to much greater time demands that tend to consume him, the "professional coach" is always trying harder than his colleagues. The real pro has a strong interest in the poorly skilled students, in his physical education classes, and spends extra time with those who may not be so interested. The poorly skilled and those not possessing a great interest can be your potential supporters in the future.

Another important aspect of the coach's job is to sell the good that is taking place. To focus on accomplishments often meets deaf and nonunderstanding ears. It is important to meet faculty on their own ground and enjoy them for what they are. Know what they have for interests. You then may be on your way to developing a friend. A friend will be much more apt to support your work. In turn, your friend will perhaps get to know a bit more about what you are doing. Like other humans, when they *ask* they are really ready to learn.

One must appreciate the fact that misunderstanding is a natural phenomenon. Often, other faculty are not familiar with your role. *There is also a tendency for faculty to view everyone's role in light of their own position.* This often leads to criticism. To say the coach and physical educator are nonacademic, second class faculty is easy. It is academic snobbery when a faculty ignores the physical education teacher when he is dressed down for his gym teaching. I have observed many coaches being ignored when dressed down to teach and accepted when they are attending the faculty functions. It is interesting but sad. Meet faculty on their own ground for more understanding and support.

Do many coaches not do a good teaching job in their physical education classes? Why?

Have you noted that many coaches who have good faculty relations, sell their programs well, and do a good teaching job in their physical education classes?

What are other ways you can create better relationships with the faculty?

INGREDIENTS FOR MEDIOCRITY EXIST
IN OUR SCHOOL SYSTEM

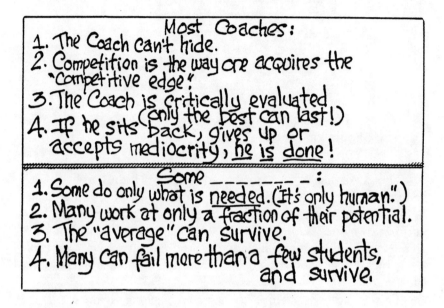

Most Coaches:
1. The Coach can't hide.
2. Competition is the way one acquires the "competitive edge."
3. The Coach is critically evaluated (only the best can last!)
4. If he sits back, gives up or accepts mediocrity, <u>he is done</u>!

Some _____:
1. Some do only what is <u>needed</u>. ("It's only human.")
2. Many work at only a fraction of their potential.
3. The "average" can survive.
4. Many can fail more than a few students, and survive.

One may question the dedication of a few coaches. One may also question the dedication and commitment of many of our classroom teachers. The major contributing factor is not having to be as competitive. The individual hours and the collective hours given to students by the classroom teacher is less. Teachers are not as critically evaluated. It is human to do only what is needed. Many potentially top quality teachers are working at a fraction of their potential. A teacher may "hide" in the day-to-day routine. We have alluded to the competitive aspect the coach deals with. He also has another factor that keeps him on his toes. Hundreds and even thousands are watching and evaluating the coach. He is often unfairly evaluated.

"There's One At Every Game"

He stalks the gridiron every year
Old varsity jacket — and belly of beer;

He was the greatest when he played ball.
A coach, a player — he knew it all.
He rips the boys, beats down the coach.
A perfect jackass with his approach.
"No blocking, no passing, no defense at all!"
The loud mouth slob is taking a shot at it all.
Toward his Alma Mater he's really true.
"They stink" — he shouts, as the game is through.
He wends his way up to the coach
And with a glassy stare —
Shouts loud for all the stands to hear,
"You're out, bub — have no fear."

The coach has to have a lot more going for him than "average" to survive. If he fails with more than a very few of his athletes, he is down with his ship right now. But, you are lucky your field is a competitive one. Competition is how one maintains the competitive edge. The coach also usually has a compulsive drive — he can't be happy if he does not coach. Therefore, athletics has another plus.

This is not an attempt to degrade teaching. I am a lifelong teacher in the classroom. This is an attempt to objectively compare the two roles in the educational picture.

We all have observed the unfair competition many coaches have to live with. What can be done about the few coaches that are not competitive by nature of their approach?

THOSE AGAINST ATHLETICS

There are three categories of people, particularly faculty, that pass judgment on physical education and athletics. Of course, this varies a lot from one situation to another, but here are some of the feelings the author has experienced.

There are some people that basically are against sport or physical education. They arrive at this position because of past experience — or *lack of experience.* That person is often without exposure and, therefore, does not value your field. He lived without it and feels it is just a frill that others do not need. Just as people defend what they do, so often do those that have no exposure.

Then there is a small group that have had a *poor experience* and feel all sport or physical education is bad. For example, if one had a coach that did a poor job and as a participant he got "hurt" in some way, he then feels all sport is of little value. There are some that, unfortunately, have had poor experiences — leadership usually being the cause, not sport conditions themselves. Some can sort out the difference, while others may not be able to.

Last — and there are a lot of these — they like to be controversial. At every gathering, they like to speak out. They oppose what is proposed. It is very easy to find negative people, disenchanted people, those only expecting to meet up with the perfect *ideal,* expecting one to *"walk on water,"* accepting absolutely no flaws, expecting everything in one perfect package. They debate whatever is proposed.

Our field is not immune. The same kind of thing happens when a physical educator is overly critical of Little League or Flag Football. He downs all of the good because an ideal in his mind is not being met. He would be far more humanistic if he was for sports programs of this nature; then if they seem to have glaring weaknesses, concentrate on trying to help change the situation so that it becomes an all-around powerful and positive force for youngsters.

There is still another force against athletics and it has been alluded to before. There are some community members, regardless of inflation or good times, that will always vote "no" to any proposed cost increase in taxes regardless of how justified. Money, for one reason or another, seems to be their obsession, the most important thing to them. Further, for some people this is a definite reality. Retired people on fixed income is an example.

Does it help to know what your opposition may be like? Perhaps it does not help much, as these individuals will continue to think as they do. They will defend their positions without being able to understand most arguments. Either they do not want to try to understand or their value judgments are very strong. They somehow do not seem to be able to comprehend the values for youngsters engaged in sport.

What can you do? Perhaps concentrate on your supporters. They are the "doing" people. However, if you establish friendships with the nonbelievers, they may well accept what you are doing. Having nothing but fine comments coming from those participating is sort of convincing to those that are not *entirely* negative.

How many times have you observed those against athletics?
Have you sorted out their reasons?
What are other reasons?

Chapter 5

THE SPECIFICS

WHAT TO TEACH

HAVE you ever observed a junior high or high school basketball game and watched the beginning youngsters make repeated mistakes? They have not yet had enough exposure to the right fundamentals (skills vital to successful play). Perhaps we can also say that sometimes coaches have failed to emphasize the basics, and therefore simple mistakes are continually repeated. Dribbling too high and having the ball stolen over and over again is common – yet easy for the coach to emphasize. How about the pass from one athlete to the other under the basket? Is it at chest level where it is easy to handle or is it at the knees and like a bullet? Are basic defensive positions kept in mind, basic body position so that weight can be shifted easily, with arms up? Do the athletes spread out and get open for a pass or all cluster and stand? Do they pass instead of shoot, unless they have a good shot? Does the athlete go toward the ball when it is passed to him? Going to the ball when receiving a pass is another example of a fundamental. What is stressed here is that any coach can think about the mistakes that youngsters are making and isolate them in an interesting manner. This is isolating fundamentals. The coach can then drill the isolated components in different situations so that at game time the athletes do more of the right things. Most coaches probably cover the proper fundamentals, but many fail to expose their athletes to adequate emphasis. A good coach has a better idea of what needs work. Not enough young coaches branch out with a confidence to do the things most needed. Be sure you spend enough time isolating the fundamentals – fundamentals are anything from mental concentration to finger control on the ball.

Scout your own club. Many otherwise fine coaches miss on this point. They are too busy scouting someone else or planning strategy.

When a pro loses a fundamental, he goes back and isolates his problem and works until it is flawless; then he gets it together with movement and then competition. The mark of a pro is that he does not lose his fundamentals under stress. He makes fewer mistakes. The average athlete loses his fundamentals under stress. He makes more mistakes. This is why a coach may say that the team making the fewest mistakes wins. A good athlete has to be able to apply the needed fundamentals. He has to know his strengths, know his competition, and has to believe in exactly what he has to do. The coach's job is to teach the qualities mentioned in the right blend. To focus on the athletes for mistakes on the day of competition really goes right back to the coach and *how* he prepared his squad. The good coach sorts out errors and causes and works on them during the week. At game time he concentrates on positive game administration.

Never let up on your study of body movement. Applying mechanical principles to every sport you observe will aid in your comprehension of movement patterns. You can grow throughout your *entire* coaching career. You will continually get better at isolating new fundamental skills and applying them in the right blend during practices to make more effective athletes.

How often have you observed a coach teaching but not leveling with himself?

Has he asked, "Do I have a really sound reason for teaching this particular skill at this particular time and circumstance?

What are neglected fundamentals in your sport?

How much emphasis in early, mid, and late season goes to fundamentals?

CHANGING A TECHNIQUE

1. The Coach must be sure he is right in asking an athlete to change a skill.
2. Give the athlete reasons.
3. Be sure the athlete has visualized properly.
4. He/she should then _want_ to change.
5. Break the skills down to the simplest fundamentals.
6. Practice skills full Go and relaxed.
7. Over Learn the skill.

As an athlete, the author was exposed to some top-notch teachers of systems of play. In addition, many of these coaches had every other asset going for them that was needed — interpersonal relationships, knowledge, confidence, organization, excellence in game administration, and many other pluses. Some of the coaches, however, could have given some time to reason out with the athlete why he was being asked to change an old and proven way of doing things. This point especially is increasingly important when an athlete has had another first rate coach and knows his own strengths. He feels that his fundamentals are correct. Due to experiences of this nature that I had as an athlete, much emphasis is intended here for the need for explanations of the right kind. As a coach, I tried to feel supersensitive to how the athlete feels in this kind of situation.

It is common for a coach to teach his system, his fundamentals, by just telling the athlete what he wants. On some levels, this approach is adequate. But even on all levels, some reasons have to be given. To have the athlete "not to reason why, just do or die," is creating an unthinking athlete. It is true that time and large squad numbers often contribute to this dilemma of not always giving adequate reasons for what is asked. But nonetheless, there are often many opportunities that are overlooked by the coach. The coach can gain more individual loyalty, confidence, and actual learning if he justifies his changes.

A major component of good teaching involves motivating the learner. If the following procedure is adhered to, greater learning as well as confidence will come to the athlete. There are many right ways to do something. Give some time motivating the athlete and show him exactly what is wanted and why he needs to change.

The author never has seen an outlined procedure for changing a technique, but out of a need to do a better teaching job, the following procedure was developed and applied whenever needed. More objectivity will be added to coaching, as well as getting more lasting results.

1. The coach must not teach out of tradition or by what has been taught at the expense of his *really knowing that what he is asking the athlete to do is definitely right*. A coach has to be objective and seek the truth. He must be convinced that it is right for the athlete in order to improve his skill. To say "we block this way in our system" may never really get the experienced athlete to your corner if his other techniques have

worked well for him in the past. The alert coach could well let
the athlete keep his old skill for certain specific uses. To change
the stroke of a swimmer without being completely sure that it
will make him more streamlined, relaxed, or efficient is "tam-
pering," not coaching. *Don't be "automatic" with your words;
be sure and sincere.*

2. This leads to the second aspect. *Reasons for change must be
   given* to the athlete. The athlete will be better if he truly
   believes that what he is being asked to do is *definitely right* for
   the situation. Convince him that by doing something differently, he will be better. Your conversation will center around
   sound scientific principles. It is true that this process takes
   some time and effort and at times some lengthy discussion.
   The right approach for the athlete in question is vital. You
   may have to schedule some informal meeting time with the
   athlete because you want his every loyalty. The athlete deserves
   whatever time is required for communication and understanding, no matter how busy you may be. He should then be ready
   for change.

3. The next step — assuming proper foundation and explanation
   — is *being sure that the athlete has visualized exactly what you
   want.* Remember, words often have different meanings because
   of different experiences. Pictures, motion analysis on film, and
   video tape of the athlete are excellent — demonstrations and
   critique are better than just words.

4. *The athlete should now want to do what you have asked* with
   complete dedication. He understands why he is asked to do
   something differently and visualizes how he can improve.

5. Then *the coach must be able to break the skill or skills down
   into simpler* segments or simpler fundamentals to the extent
   necessary for proper mastery. This part of the process again
   requires a sound mechanical analysis.

6. There must be opportunity to *practice the skills both in full go
   and in situations where the athlete is more relaxed.* Learning
   oftentimes comes when the athlete is not so intense, and
   sometimes it occurs the other way around. For example, if an
   athlete is very intense and hard working, he may drive himself

very hard and overlook the forest for the trees. Also, sometimes relaxation lets learning happen by different nerve and muscular input.

7. *The skill must then be overlearned.* You must provide opportunity to go back to the basic component you are emphasizing. Remember that even pros lose their skills, and when they do, they break them down until they are flawless and can be incorporated into a highly competitive situation. Whenever possible, if you follow the procedure, you will gain respect by the thinking athletes, accomplish a needed task, and have a closer bond to your team members.

Have you observed coaches who were not sensitive to the athlete's thinking process? Perhaps they did not gain maximum benefit from their teaching.

Were you ever moved to a new playing position without explanation?

How much time (maximum and minimum) could be involved in selling a new way to an athlete in your sport?

When might a coach not be able to be this detailed?

What are shortcuts to reach the athlete?

THE RIGHT CHALLENGE

There are problems within most athletic schedules. Both individual athletes and teams must be challenged at the right levels for optimum development. Continual inferior caliber competition does not sharpen skills. Perhaps a scrimmage against weaker competition helps install confidence in an offense, but to be challenged slightly above one's ability promotes the "competitive edge." Competing often in like activity and in off-season also promotes the competitive edge in athletics. It is the coach's job to try to have good competition. Perhaps a 50-50 schedule would be ideal, where the wins would come with a challenge, and the losses would occur when the squad was not outclassed.

Confidence is not fostered by continual losses. If winning occurs all of the time, a false sense of actual worth can also exist. The right balance in scheduling has a great bearing on outcomes.

Coaches often have little to say about their schedules, and many situations are real challenges. The schedule may present a losing front and attitude, or the schedule may be balanced with too many wins and/or pressures. Knowing what your prospective new job has traditionally shown in this regard could indicate the future trend to the would be applicant. The decision you make, as you enter a new position, has to seriously consider this aspect. Know the factors that can change and those that probably cannot. You will be a happier and more successful coach.

Ever see athletes in the wrong competitive setting?

Ever see a coach in the "wrong" situation?

THE ISSUE OR THE PERSON

Every team has rules. Most every squad will also experience a conflict. What does the coach do when there is a problem? The easy way is to treat it all as black or white. The rule is there, the penalty known, and the penalty given. Coach, regardless of your present attitudes, you may change as you gain experience. Life is not a matter of black and white, good or bad. There are so many variables that proper discipline, to be fair, must deal in the gray area. The intent, as well as the surrounding circumstance, are part of any broken rule.

When a problem exists, what does the coach do? Let's say a youngster is late for the bus. The coach decides to teach people a lesson and drive off on the minute outlined. There is no problem — *except* that not everyone benefits from this decision. The youngsters themselves, if asked, may not want to leave a teammate — regardless of whether that person is going to play an important or an insignificant role. Also, there is the problem of how the youngster himself looks at it after being left behind. How about the reason behind being late?

A way to destroy a boy is to relive the following experience. A college football bus drove off after a few minutes wait. The youngster that was late got a ride and made the destination along with the bus. He came to the coach with his apology. But he did not play that afternoon, and that particular game in his hometown meant a lot to him. It was disastrous to his goals for that season — and by the mistake of his alarm not going off. Does the athlete feel the same about the coach? Did the team benefit? Was learning enhanced by staying with the outlined decision? If there is a negative answer, perhaps a different solution could have been applied. The idea of discipline is to seek fair and just conclusions based on good common sense. The coach should seek appraisal of all the circumstances and make it a learning atmosphere for the boy and squad. It would have taken only a few minutes of time. This is not to negate the proposition that a coach's job is to place as much discipline on his group as he feels he can and still have good morale.

I grew up when discipline with unwavering consequences was the only goal. We left on time regardless. The coach did not allow for a few minutes delay. But as time went on in my coaching career, it seemed that there was more room for helping things go smoothly that day instead of hurting the individual and the squad. Later on, and very soon, reemphasize the problem. Do not misinterpret. If this sort of thing is hindering and hurting discipline in any way, it is time to give ample warning and leave on time. The answer to this depends on the squad, its size, the coach, and what the coach feels is most important. Not everyone looks at things just like the coach does. He must give on some points and then gain on others.

The same thing could be applied to a youngster being late for practice. If there seems to be a flimsy excuse, that is one thing. It is quite another if there are good reasons. The coach can easily alienate if he is not careful. He should work toward having his athletes take on a greater responsibility. A lot depends on the length of the season – long seasons have to be more flexible. Perhaps, rather than a sharp discipline that the youngster does not fully care for, which oftentimes is a less effective way of changing his attitudes, the coach may want to talk personally to him and the squad. Do not misunderstand – there is a time to lay into a group getting sloppy, but remember the coach has a part. If he wants his squad warmed up on their own and ready at a certain time, it is better to set an earlier time to arrive at practice, say fifteen minutes early, and settle for a varied warmup, rather than be upset when some arrive too late to get in a warmup.

The boy who breaks training rules often falls into the following categories. He can be sacrificed so that no others will dare or he can possibly be brought along by individual conversation and taking the necessary steps to help him. I have never met a youngster, when he was caught breaking training, that was not in your hand. If you fire him, you lose him and your chance to make him grow, and the squad gets hurt by losing his services. He is often your two year old stallion. You cannot give ground and let it repeat. Just be sure you have given him and the squad a chance to benefit. There is a great deal to be said about this and I risk being misunderstood. Discipline is essential, and it is something that grows only when rules are observed. However, the best conduct is out of loyalty. An understanding and respected coach helps. One mistake should not ruin a boy or a team. I grew the most when I was helped after making mistakes.

The hard and fast routine was brought home to me at a church-related college where I coached. Alcohol, among other things, was forbidden on campus. An athlete tried alcohol for the first time in a fraternity house. When it was known that there was a party of this kind, the youngsters involved were sought out. One youngster was not named. The young man, being honest, stepped forth and volunteered his part – he was trying a can of beer for the first time. Another young lad was married and had made a great sacrifice to attend college. However, the president made it clear that these were rules and anyone found guilty would be expelled – no exceptions. It would appear to me that at a church affiliated school, trying to forgive, trying to save, and trying to do a teaching job so the outcomes would be lasting would be more appropriate than crucifying a person for this sort of "dastardly crime." When a youngster leaves school, married or not, he has to make some major readjustments that are hard financially, and there is a scar on progress toward his career. All this was unnecessary if the individual was the main concern. Isn't that the idea? Good discipline means treating everyone fairly but differently and making one grow because of it. These young men were fine people, and what they did in no way affected their ability or character. I have reservations, however, about the superiors that passed the harsh and poor judgments on them. Understanding, compassion, good judgment, counseling, and showing one the right way are part of "saving" and should have been a part of the makeup of people in responsible positions. Sydney Harris, a syndicated columnist, brought it all home when he was quoted in the early 60s in an Adrian, Michigan, newspaper: "The saints with the most meaning for humanity are those who fought and won their way to virtue and thus know what a precarious state it is, and how vulnerable even the best of us can be. The real saints have all been ex-sinners." I think that era relating to the church-related school's discipline is past, but coaches often are a party to similarly limiting the use of their gray matter. At any rate, you'll have your chances to be a participant.

The fine line of good judgment cannot be taught by reading a text. It is more of an acquired quality that comes slowly by an "osmotic" process. Perhaps the most lacking thing on college campuses today is this very thing. Professors and administrators lack time in the "concrete." Perhaps if they worked more with their hands, hard physical work, and experienced a more varied life, they would know how to look at things more realistically. It is hard to spend all of one's life in a "tower" and still be able to be very much in touch with life on the ground.

The discussion of this area is endless and seldom agreed upon as every athletic team is different as is every athlete and every

coach. The need for varied *experiences and resourcefulness* comes
forth as discipline problems arise.

How many situations have you observed where discipline was
improperly handled?

State your philosophy on the many areas you will have to en-
counter.

What are some variables that may change your thinking?

AN ASSET TO ANY COACH

After discussing discipline, this topic seems appropriate. It
must be in the right mixture – humility. What makes this fine
quality? To be able to laugh at oneself comes to those who are
sure of themselves and have a real knowledge of just where they
fit into the world. The kind of men that know all the trees, birds,
animals, and plants in their environment, because they have lived
close to nature, are not the kind that thrive on their own importance. Perhaps this is not a fair example for all situations. I am
sure there are many factors possible. But, let's look at it another

way. It is commonplace to observe people in their professional lives attach great importance to their roles and to themselves. Why? Their conduct is often unattractive. It has often been said, "A man all wrapped up in himself makes a pretty small package." Arthur Godfrey, *McCall's Magazine,* November 1959, emphasizes this point when he states, "The impression left behind by most of us usually just about equals the hole left in a bucket of water after a clenched fist is withdrawn." In contrast to those fortunate enough to be in coaching, an administrator can shift the blame, "reorganize," move people around in different roles, and feel he is on top of everything around him. He might typically have an arrogant attitude. Again, why? This same man is easily outlcassed by mother nature as well as being outwitted by many lower forms of animal life. Within nature, there is no need or place for overbearance. The same scheme should exist in one's work life — it would if we were all mature. The difference lies in "real" experience — not necessarily in nature. Are those real of the administrator? How about the coach who is winning consistently over a period of time. Is he having a "real" experience? I doubt it. It is so easy for him to forget humility, to lose the grasp on some things because he is "fat, dumb and happy," like the athlete who has had a lot of success and yet not been stung with defeat. Fortunately, games are like crises and most coaches know what it is to lose. The coach often learns that there is a time for humility just as there is a definite need for complete confidence and decisive leadership. You are lucky if you have this quality come through at frequent and proper times. Many varied experiences can help you. At any rate, reach out for this asset. Too many people on the rise in their careers lack this great quality. You will not be the *best* until it is part of you.

You all have come in contact with the person lacking this important quality.

Perhaps it is more appropriate to list the great men that possess this asset.

VARIETY AND ROUTINE

The sport season can be very long. Variety, even in the short seasons, makes the day to day work fun. Listening to your athletes' input is valuable to variety. Try offering some practices that are not exactly what you feel is needed, but what the athletes like. They will work extra hard. You may accomplish more in the end. Printing out each practice so that everyone can have a copy may be quite worthwhile. The athlete can figure how he might get the most out of the session. I have tried giving practices both ways and ended up letting them know what is coming. The thinking athlete can benefit much more if he knows where he can adjust to his specialty and where he might put in his best effort. He is oriented before he starts practice — a good way to begin anything.

Bulletin boards and thoughts for the day can help set the proper atmosphere for practice. The "saying for the day" also adds something. It all started when one of the athletes asked me, "What was the word for the day?" I started publishing a thought of a positive nature and found the practice worthwhile. Not all thoughts are original – many you have heard, as they are maxims in coaching, but here is an example of just a few:

- "A well-conditioned mind and a well-conditioned body is an unbeatable combination."
- "The enviable frame of mind for your competition is to look at it like it is your time to enjoy what you are so *well prepared* to do."
- "The team that makes the least mistakes in preparation wins."
- "Practice as if the whole team and success depends on you, because it does."
- "Team work means success – work together – win together."
- "When you commit to goals like you are this season, or like you can in life, then you immediately are experiencing the dignity of work, the satisfaction of doing something worthwhile, and pride in yourself in proportion to your effort."
- "A champion has to not only have desire to be good but has to know how to make himself work toward that goal."
- "You compete the way you practice."
- "The phrase 'good teams are made of good benches' is true. It is what everyone gives that harnesses people power. Our number three man may be our most valuable by his total contribution."
- "Whatever impedes a man but does not stop him aids him in his progress."
- "The harder you work, the more fortunate you become."
- "It is easy to give up or quit if you do not put much into what you are doing. Do not confuse this with losing gracefully, this we automatically do, just as we win graciously."
- "How you look at life is all in a state of mind. A man can be happy poor, sad a millionaire. True with any value of life. Be positive."
- "Good athletes are thinking athletes. Always be thinking how you can get better and how the team can win."

— "This is how you win:

Be a winner!
If you think you are beaten, you are;
If you think you dare not, you don't,
If you like to win, but think you can't
It's almost a cinch you won't.

If you think you'll lose, you're lost.
For out in the world we find
Success begins with a fellow's will;
It's all in the state of mind.

Life's battles don't always go
To the stronger or faster man;
But sooner or later the man who wins
Is the one who thinks he can."

— "Never do anything so that you look back and realize that you did less than your best. Those are the kind that say 'I could have been, if . . . ?'"

— "You will gain strength if you believe that no one can hurt you but you yourself and no one can help you but you yourself. Rely more on yourself in all you do. You will be stronger for it. The team will rise and fall by what *you* do."

— "Find the key. Those that are on top know how to put it together."

— "Success is a great teacher, but adversity can be greater."

— "The difference between good and great oftentimes is less than 5 percent. Give your daily work a 10 percent extra effort and see what happens."

— "Opportunity starts now, not at some unknown time in the future. Your only limitation on what you can accomplish in our society is your own ability to motivate yourself. Very few lack ability for success. Sort out what has to be done and meet your goals."

— "One of the greatest satisfactions of life can be yours when you realize that your God-given body has hit its physical potential in an athletic activity of your interest. True physical maturity, better understanding of self, added confidence and pride come with this attainment. The man who passes his youth and enters adulthood without knowing what it is like to be at his best has missed an important part of life. The flower that did not bloom."

— "Man's physical fitness and the functions it relates to has been, in the past and still is, one of his greatest assets for enjoyable living and in survival. Physical fitness may well be his and his country's greatest asset."

— "You get out of your mind what you put into it. Positive thoughts yield positive results. Only speak to others in positive terms. Good thoughts spread. Individuals and teams get stronger. Do your part today."

— "If you don't know what you want, it is a sign either that you did not seriously want it, or that you tried to bargain over the price." R. Kipling

— "When you laugh, the world laughs with you, when you cry, you cry alone."

— "An athlete without clear-cut goals is like a ship without a rudder. Only by first finding the key to your mind can a championship level be reached."

— "When a person no longer has goals, there is not much else left."

— "*YOU* can be a champion. You have to be the first to practice everyday. You have to work at being the very best on the squad. You have to learn that the team comes before your personal glory. You have to give any time the team asks. Then win or lose — *you are a champion.*"

You can purchase slogans that give you ideas. However, each day will remind you of something that needs to be said. It works. There is no limit on how many you can come up with as things are always happening to give you a thought.

The following is a typical thought for the day. I addressed the squad in 1970 before our first meet to sort of set the stage for the beginning of the season.

"As I make up the practice schedule on this last practice before our first meet — the way you have lent yourself to work for so long this fall brings some thoughts to mind that I want to share with you.

All of a sudden it is the beginning of my twentieth year of coaching. Already this squad is developing its character as a unit — it seems to typify the best of all the sports and teams I have had. Things are happening and some specific thoughts that are a part of my life, never to be taken away, come to mind.

Here is my place, and yours, where we both leave the tensions of the day. Even though it is life seen clear and concentrated with all its problems and heartaches, it is more happiness from work, and even greater elation from outstanding performances.

It is meeting the highest type of young man connected with sport at this university. And, even more, to me, it is associating with, believe it or not, the finest in objectivity and character on campus, faculty included. There is something special down here. It is the Gross's, Mill's, Cheney's.

It is a place where loyalty is a part of life because it occurs in proportion to giving of yourself.

It is a place where I see the best conditioned bodies and minds in any sport on campus.

It is a setting where one of the greatest problems of the world today — that of getting along with others — is reduced to a common and easy solution. Never a color, social, or other barrier have I found — it is rather mutual respect from dedication and hard work. Also I have never found a young man that I have not liked, nor have I ever felt disliked.

It is a place where I see excellence demanded — the only place in the formal education process that perfection is shared as a common goal.

It is enthusiasm, positive thinking, a place of great expectations, and a place where disappointment becomes a brief interlude — never a place of defeat. It is life handled with pride, self-control, honesty, and confidence.

It is sportsmanship — win or lose — where visiting teams go away from here respecting us. We are a tough team, but also are the one they most like to swim against. All relating to the every way we treat them as our guests when they arrive, during the meet, and after in the room upstairs.

We *all* mature a little faster here. It is hard to match the coaching experience for a man.

It is Paul, Dick, and John and past team managers and captains that seem especially dedicated to making things happen — all by placing a cause above their personal gain — as you also do.

It is identifying as a group in travel. At recent banquets, we have been the only squad with our blazers and sitting together.

I think of your walking in the cold of winter to the pool, where the water may be coldish, hard on the eyes, choppy, and even the air cool. And then there is the day when it is like a new breath of life to look at the pink sunset on the mountains before stepping into the complex and to a warm clean pool for practice.

It is a beginning and sort of ending. Starting when I first met you and oftentimes your parents, following your oftentimes shaky progress on to graduation some short four years later — to see a man that I would be more than happy to call my son, and capable in every way of tackling life's problems.

It is winning that close one, and every few years the one we had no right winning that sends the chills up your back. There is no other place in life where this happens and if I have shared these thoughts as intently related to the purpose of life, I can only feel with strong conviction that this is the best way I could have spent my time."

The above thought for the day is long, but put together your thoughts for the day. It creates a good setting.

OTHER THAN SLOGANS AND BULLETIN BOARDS

The purpose of posting positive thoughts and developing bulletin boards was to create the best possible mental attitude for each squad member. There are other ways to gain positive effects. The coach can always seize on the chance to teach. A great teacher always uses an experience to bring home in a positive way something that has happened. You may believe in playing as many athletes as you can even if it is at the expense of your win-loss record. A junior high or J.V. program would be a situation where such a philosophy would be appropriate. Some of the athletes could criticize or make cruel comments to the substitutes you use. This is a chance to teach respect for a second and third stringer. These youngsters will eventually come through from experience. When they do something really well, it is time to emphasize that person's value and the factors such as having a chance to learn. This is seizing on an opportunity to teach understanding of others, individual worth, confidence, and many other things.

What else can the coach do? He can make things happen instead of having things happen, and using this experience to teach. He can, for example, have the squad believe they are in better condition because they have worked harder. It may mean the extra practice in the rain, or what a friend of mine did by starting at midnight of the first day they could begin. The athletes probably lost a lot of sleep and it did them no real good physically, but they were told that they were working while the other teams were sleeping. Confidence was instilled. The extra work can make them believe in coming through in the end. This attitude was always emphasized relative to working all the way, despite disappointments. If the squad believes that they may have lost only because they needed more time to get the score up in their favor, then you have instilled a winning attitude. "We didn't lose, we just ran out of time." They need to have alternate plans to meet disappointments, and then they will feel they can cope with anything that happens. This is an example of a coach having a lot to do with creating a positive winning attitude.

To have each one put every bit of information into the coach on how to win is another way. The minds of all men are better than just the coach's. They are urged to contribute their ideas. You are making things happen. You are directly involving your squad. They will then have a stronger part in the organization. Each will feel personally responsible for the success of the squad. The athletes become team men, closer to teammates, and they feel confident because they have harnessed their people power. The coach just has to know when to cut it off and make his decisions.

When everyone contributes, the coach can benefit too. The coach can feel comfortable by game time because he has sorted out and used every bit of input. He is less likely to experience the sin of being outcoached. Being outcoached causes many sleepless nights thereafter, and a couple or three lessons cure any coach. The higher the level of competition, the more valuable the input.

To some coaches, to let the athletes think could be less than productive. To other coaches, it would be analogous to the master teacher bringing forth talent by fostering enthusiasm and ingenuity.

How many other examples have you witnessed?

A WAY OF DEFINING WORK OUTPUT

It is well recognized by experts in body movement, physiologists, and psychologists that relaxed practices are very valuable in developing technique. The athlete is not concentrating on energy output. He is thinking about his form and working on strengths, weaknesses, and technique. However, *intensity* has to be a key word for the athlete. "The way an athlete practices is the way he plays." You have to convey this. The athlete has to believe in this work ethic. A good week often lets the coach know what he and the squad are in for on Saturday. The "die is cast." The job in preparation requires an intensity in practice. "Intensity" in effort is vital as contrasted to a nonchalant, less concentrated, or even diverted attitude. A nonthinking athlete has little learning, even though his energy output is high. A keyed up mind often denotes a keyed up body. A combination geared for competition and in many ways learning is at its maximum. How does one become an intense worker? It is very hard to say. It is partially innate. It is also partly related to his psychological image, or hero worship image, or basic need for excelling. It is also related to another factor that is related to everything, and this is a past work experience. This affects his attitude and perspective in many ways. Regardless, the job of the coach is to have the athlete realize through every means possible that intensity is vital to success, and that the nonchalant work pattern, where the mind is thinking about something else, is not a usual and productive way. Do not confuse the fact that a keyed up mind may not always mean a keyed up body. In some sports, athletes have to control the tenseness in just the right manner. Too much expressed emotion during the week may not leave any for Saturday. Teams can peak before the game. Watching the eyes and relating it to the physical output and level of accomplishment and noting the mistakes being made from over tense muscles all helps the coach. At any rate, the job is to have all get there first with their minds. The rest will work out.

Record your thinking and nonthinking athletes as they practiced and relate the outcome.

Discuss "mental practice" technique.

What are some avenues open to the coach to achieve better work output?

TO BECOME THE ATHLETE'S COACH

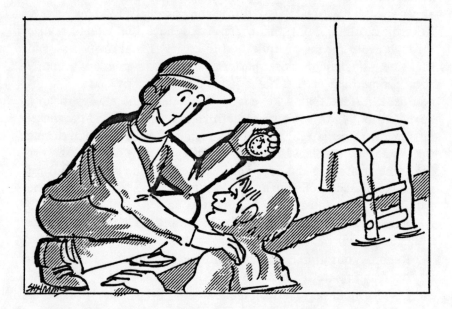

You take a giant step forward in becoming the athlete's coach when you can do something for him. In order to really be his coach, it is necessary that he experience the results he wants. This is your hold on the athlete.

In some cases, a scholarship may gain much alliance between coach and athlete. But, when the coach genuinely does something for an athlete, he has a better position than before. What is a prime example? Lowering an athlete's time in sports like track or swimming lets the athlete see the fruits of his work. This is another and most vital way to really become his coach. You have to do this or you have not arrived yet.

What are the many ways a coach can become the athlete's coach?

CONSIDERATIONS FOR LASTING SUCCESS

A few guidelines may pay big dividends. Always treat others as you would be treated. Running up scores is a practice sometimes done by a coach harboring a grudge. There is no place for that because you hurt youngsters on both teams. You are, therefore, hurting sport and in turn yourself.

To be known as an honest person is a number one consideration. The coach who uses a trick to win that involves something shady has to live with a poor image among his fellow coaches. He did not teach his athletes the right lessons either. They will be the first to see through.

Don't get caught up in polls if you can help it. This portion of the media has not helped many high school and small college contests achieve the right ends. If teams have to run up scores to be rated, values are altered. Always create respect *for another team* within your athletes.

Scheduling similar schools if at all possible can be a consideration for lasting success. Conference rules help teams gain strength, and the good of the league should be a foremost thought for all of the league members' long-term goals. This approach actually helps every team's position. Oftentimes, coaches on the top want to break away from the rules of the league to schedule a class above. Over the long-term, it could not be the right move.

To use the phrase that "nice guys do win" and to bring this kind of idea home as often as possible is an additional consideration for lasting success. To make your program strong enough so that you do not have to sweat the "small stuff" is an easy way to go about it all.

Don't allow any athlete to get away with any kind of action you feel is unbecoming to your goals. He, as well as you, must always be aboveboard.

Have as your coaching goal to "weather" well — gain fellowship and respect from your fellow coaches. *If they can say that you are a competitor and a gentleman, that's it.* You've made it as the kind of person you like yourself, and your athletes will be attracted to what you have to offer.

List the elite coaches that fulfilled this ideal.

Discuss where coaches failed who were not good competitors and gentlemen.

OBSERVING RESPECT

If you can observe your athletes helping their JV counterparts, your program is in good shape. If, on the other hand, you observe backhanded comments regarding how they are doing when the varsity is watching them perform, there is a lack of respect in the program. I once observed a two year turnabout in this coaching aspect. The coach who was in his last year had not done things much like a professional, and I can vividly remember many of the varsity squad watching a JV game and laughing at their mistakes. A couple of years later some of those same varsity athletes attended the JV games and helped each JV, which was a great change to observe. And all is coming from the way you teach, out of respect, and seizing an opportunity to teach for the right outcomes.

The same observation can be made as you review your practice or game film. An undisciplined squad will laugh at mistakes – a disciplined squad is focused and intent on learning.

The athlete that comes to practice faithfully even when he is injured is paying respect to the program. The alert coach seizes on this and helps others gain more respect for the program. You have to teach for it to gain it.

Think of the many ways coaches have missed on this point. Also recall the examples of those that did it right.

WHAT GOALS?

Every coach has personal goals. What kind? A common goal is one of great ambition. Perhaps it includes his eventually coaching at a very prestigious institution. At any rate, his present position, he discovers, is much less than he had hoped for. His loyalty may be challenged. It is common to give in and not support your superiors. Forget it. It isn't worth it. No one wants to hear sour grapes. Be loyal, strong, and enthused, but leave. Then speak your mind if you wish. This above example is often a coach's great challenge. Remember, it is common for *less than appealing* coaching situations to exist.

So you want the top? Winning records are vital. It is easy to get things out of perspective and forget the real job of the coach.

What is prestige? Is it being at a larger institution? Does this situation best utilize your talents and does it give maximum satisfaction? Is it money? Perhaps your goals lie with each individual athlete you have — seeing him grow and do well after he leaves your program. If so, you may best do this in high school. Those are formative years. You also have more "personal touch" time in smaller programs. Be sure you have the right goals for you.

Game conduct is a neglected goal of many. I have watched some coaches berate their athletes for making mistakes. They forget it is really their fault for not defining talent, the raw components of what had to be taught, and then going about teaching effectively.

There are two appropriate goals that can make a coach happy with his coaching career. Have a team so well prepared, mentally and physically, that they want to show the other teams that they are tough and want to perform regardless of how difficult the task is. They want the other team to have the *GREATEST RESPECT* for them. The greatest respect over all other teams that their opponents may meet. A well prepared team is going to give any opponent a hard time before they go under — this gains respect. And, second, if they are *THE KIND OF TEAM THAT OTHERS MOST LIKE TO MEET,* as there is a little extra class there, you have it all together. Just as a well conditioned mind in a well conditioned body is an unbeatable combination, so it is with a team. They will win their share of close ones over the years. This has nothing to do with your burning desire to create a winner, to get to the top. The two concepts are compatible.

What are your goals?

EVALUATION TO IMPROVE INSTRUCTION

Evaluation is necessary in order to create the most effective individual and the best possible program. There is a tendency when money is easily available, when winning occurs, just to continue with a satisfied approach. Coaches often observe athletes enjoying the "fat, dumb, and happy syndrome" after successes. It can be disastrous. Coaches, too, are subject to the same pitfalls, perhaps only on a longer continuum.

Peer evaluation can help the coach; so, too, can evaluation from the athletes be very informative. Either way, or both, it is stimulation and helps the coach. Peer evaluation could take many forms. Observations set up for that purpose is one method. Meetings with frank exchange is another. However, in order for this to take place, a solid level of competence and confidence first has to exist; for example, even college faculty have to be around each other a while and feel very comfortable about their teaching jobs before they entertain the pleasure of having some of their peers criticize their teaching. The second method is perhaps easier to do — getting together and talking frankly about what they think.

Player evaluation is perhaps a less mature source, but it does get to the grass roots of what athletes think. This kind of evaluation has to become a vital part of the coach and how he administers his program. There are many evaluative procedures, but better than just writing what the athlete has on his mind, a form, if properly prepared and that is not suggestive along any one area, can be of tremendous help. The following is what I feel a good example of a young coach trying to learn *all* he can about his coaching, as well as what the athletes think about the program. (This evaluation appeared in *Collegiate Baseball,* Vol. XXIV No. 10, May 15, 1981, Pg. 6). The second evaluation outline is for player evaluation. The player also should benefit from taking a look at himself in light of some of the qualities that are important to his becoming a good athlete. If some of the qualities do not jibe with how the coach perceives things, there is an additional something to be learned. The latter aspect can be of particular benefit to both the player and the coach.

Evaluation of the Coach and the UVM Baseball Program

Carefully examine the following scale. Read the questions carefully, and in the space provided after each question, indicate the most exact number that best represents your response to that question. Please be honest and think out your responses carefully.

This rating scale pertains to the following questions 1-40.

SCALE: 10   9   8   7   6 5 4   3   2   1
        excellent/very good/good/above/+ avg.-/below/fair/poor/very poor
                    avg.   avg.

___ 1. In terms of enjoyment, how would you rate our overall baseball program here at UVM?

___ 2. How do you feel about the time and effort I expect from you?

___ 3. Rate your overall satisfaction of what you are getting out of the UVM baseball program compared to what you anticipated you might when you first enrolled here.

___ 4. How do you feel our program is improving?

___ 5. If you were talking to a prospective college player in high school that was interested in our baseball program, what word would you use to describe our program to him?

___ 6. Rate *your* understanding of where our UVM baseball program is heading (our goals).

___ 7. How would you rate our team discipline expectations in relation to what you think should be expected from college athletes?

___ 8. How would you assess our overall team discipline?

___ 9. Assess my effort as far as trying to do everything possible for the betterment of the team.

___10. Assess *your* understanding of what I expect from you in terms of effort in practices and games.

___11. Rate my ability to lead by example in terms of hard work, dedication, and loyalty.

___12. How would you rate my enthusiasm?

___13. How would you rate me in terms of my honesty with you?

___14. Rate my friendliness.

___15. Rate my sense of humor as a positive quality.

___16. How would you rate me in terms of fairness with you?

___17. Rate my cheerfulness.

___18. Assess my sensitivity to the needs of the players.

___19. Rate my concern for player morale.

___20. Rate my adaptability and flexibility traits.

___21. Assess my ability to face conflict and handle it.

___22. Assess my ability to motivate you and get the best out of you and your effort.

___23. Rate my ability to "psych you up" or mentally prepare you for games.

___24. I am an emotional person. What kind of influence does that have on you?

___25. Rate my ability to get the best out of you in any situation.

___26. Rate my knowledge about the techniques involved in baseball.

___27. Rate my knowledge about the strategy involved in baseball.

___28. Rate my knowledge and ability concerning the use of personnel in our program.

___29. Assess my ability and consistency to put the right players in the lineup.

___30. Rate my ability to put you in situations that challenge and test your capabilities.

___31. Assess my *effort* to provide you with individual attention.

___32. Rate my ability to teach the fundamentals of baseball.

___33. Assess my ability to demonstrate as a valuable learning and teaching tool.

__ 34. Assess my ability to explain and correct both technique and fundamentals.

__ 35. During game situations, how would you rate my ability to "make the right moves" in terms of strategy?

__ 36. Assess my overall judgment concerning all decisions having to be made by the coach.

__ 37. Rate my overall ability as a coach for our particular situation here at UVM.

__ 38. Rate me in comparison to your opinions and impressions of those coaches we come up against.

__ 39. How would you assess the mixture of our friend-coach relationship?

__ 40. In general, how do you think I am doing my job as coach of the UVM baseball team?

Questions 41-50 pertain to the following scale. Read each question carefully and write in the number from the scale that best represents your response to the question.

SCALE:

10	9	8	7	6	5	4	3	2	1
always		most of the time		+sometimes-			rarely		never

__ 41. Do I work hard enough for you and our program?

__ 42. Do I give you as much effort as I expect out of you?

__ 43. Do you ever wish you had gone to a different college because of baseball?

__ 44. Do you look forward to going to practices and working hard?

__ 45. Do I make you feel like you are an important part of the team?

__ 46. Do you feel free to come to talk to me about anything you may want to whether or not it has to do with baseball?

__ 47. Do you get enough personal attention considering time, number of players, and number of coaches available?

__ 48. Am I open enough to player suggestions and needs?

__ 49. Are practices well organized so that everyone is working hard to improve?

__ 50. Do you believe that we are practicing the right things in order to reach our successful team goals?

Short Answer Questions

List any things that you feel might help to improve our program.

List any things you think I could be doing better as coach.

List any things you particularly like about the job I am doing as coach.

Self-evaluation by the Players

NAME_____

Carefully examine the following scale. Read the questions carefully and in the space provided after each question, indicate the most exact number that best represents your response to that question. Please be honest with yourself and think out your responses carefully.

This rating scale pertains to the following questions 1-15.

SCALE:

10	9	8	7	6	5	4	3	2	1
excellent		good		+		-		poor	
	very good		above avg.	average		below avg.		very	poor

___ 1. How would you assess your overall daily effort during practices this fall?

___ 2. How would you assess your overall improvement during the fall baseball season?

___ 3. Rate your mental preparation for practices each day.

___ 4. How would you rate your ability to assume a leadership role during practices and games?

___ 5. During any lag time in practice, rate your effort to work on drills to improve yourself as a baseball player.

___ 6. Assess your overall *team* attitude.

___ 7. If everyone on the team possessed the desire, motivation, attitude, and ability to push themselves that you have, what kind of team would we have?

___ 8. Describe your ability in comparison to the competition at your position.

___ 9. Assess your extra-*effort* (Example: practicing on your own before or after practice).

___10. Assess your effort in trying to know and be friendly with each individual out practicing.

___11. Assess your ability to keep from making the same mistake twice.

___12. Rate your effort in trying to help out others on the team as well as those trying out for your position.

___13. Assess your consistency in terms of effort in practice each day.

___14. Assess your consistency as a player in practice each day.

___15. What kind of an example do you set for others to follow?

Read carefully the following questions and respond with the number that best represents your feelings to that question.

Questions 16-23 pertain to the following scale:

SCALE:

10	9	8	7	6	5	4	3	2	1
always		most of the time		+ sometimes -			rarely		never

__16. How often do you push yourself past the expected level of effort during practices?

__17. How often do you depend on the coach to motivate and push you?

__18. Was your effort during practices this fall more than those competing for your position?

__19. Were you open to, and did you accept, the new techniques taught to you this fall?

__20. Did you ever miss a practice because of poor academic planning?

__21. Here at UVM, have you ever been more concerned with individual statistics than the success of the team?

__22. Looking back over the fall, how often did you let one mistake lead to another?

__23. Do you represent the University of Vermont team as expected both on and off the field?

Questions 24-27 can be answered with a yes or no response. Circle the appropriate response and briefly explain your answer if you feel it is necessary.

24. Can you look back over the fall and say you progressed as much as you were capable of?

                                                    YES   NO

Explain:

25. Are you at all times a good example for others on the team to follow?

                                                    YES   NO

Explain:

26. Are you capable of making more of a contribution to the team than you showed this fall?

                                                    YES   NO

Explain:

27. Was your attitude and effort this fall indicative of your potential?

                                                    YES   NO

Explain:

Questions 28-31 involve a well thought out short answer response.

28. What are some abilities, qualities, or characteristics that you have that might be more positive than those trying out for your position?

29. What are some things you feel you need to improve on to earn a starting position over competition?

30. What are some things you could have done better in looking over the fall (Example: effort, consistency and specific parts of your game)?

31. What are some key differences in the things I expect from you as compared to what has been expected from you in the past from your other baseball coaches?

32. Feel free to write any additional comments.

Carefully look through the following descriptive words or phrases. Circle *five* of the words or phrases that you feel *best* describe *you* as a baseball player here at UVM.

tough	intense	extra-effort
winner	leader	consistent
competitive	unsure	potential
relaxed	confident	always mentally ready
110%	dedicated	inconsistent
follower	smooth	make the great play
improved	satisfied	loyal
best at your position	a believer	off and on
aggressive	motivated	a good example
tense		

To be able to look at oneself objectively is very difficult. This is why a *complete* and *suggested* questionnaire seems most appropriate. The player self-evaluation is an attempt to improve on the most important asset an athlete has — his mental assets.

Are there other methods of evaluation that appeal to you?

Perhaps you could improve on your present techniques of evaluation?

If you do not have any criteria developed, perhaps a new document for evaluation would be helpful.

Chapter 6

COMMON AND UNCOMMON CONCERNS

DEALING WITH SUPERIORS AND THE PUBLIC

A very important component of success is that of having the right kind of relationships with those that are directly or indirectly allied with your program. Knowing what to say, being able to speak with good diction, and being totally sincere is a tremendous asset. Knowing when to talk and when to listen, when to be strong and when to give in, or saying "I don't know" is also a great asset. These attributes separate an articulate, widely accepted, and respected person from one in the "rough." It is what contributes greatly to being a professional person versus one who displays an unprofessional image. However, to always say the right thing at the right time belongs to only a few. Perhaps the advantage goes to the older coach. He has experience. He is often able to be more perceptive, having missed golden opportunities in the past.

It certainly is possible to be a great coach and not be a great speaker or even be very articulate in a social way. However, if one starts with being competent and hard working, caring, and doing a good job, this sincerity is becoming.

Because the coach spends so much of his life in a specific area, it is natural to become articulate.

What makes a good public speaker? Preparation. Even if you are doing just one thing for your life's work, you need preparation to properly address a group. I once had great pleasure hearing a minister who was "super" every week. He was one of the top five speakers I ever heard. He knew just what to say. He also knew just when to stop. He knew how to appeal to fact and emotion. His success formula? "I spend about thirty hours for every forty five minutes I speak." This is what it takes. I also recall a statement made to me by a journalist friend. "I may get more productive with time, but it is not what I write, it is what I rewrite." Preparation again makes the winner. Part of good preparation is knowing when to finish. This is why you probably can count on one hand the great speakers you have heard in a lifetime.

The point to be made is that it is valuable to be able to communicate with all facets concerned — it sells your program and you. Even though it's natural due to your concentrated efforts with youngsters, it takes effort in advance to come across at your best. Work at this aspect. It is vital to you and your sport.

How many otherwise fine coaches have you met that missed on this point?

Recall the few coaches that had it "together" on this aspect.

SORTING OUT MATERIAL

The real skills needed to win are often not analyzed properly and reemphasized at the right time along the way. Here is an example. Coaches at a large university went to observe the number one team in the country. They returned home and incorporated the other team's drills in their practice programs. The ideas were good in many cases, but the borrowed drills did not stress the fundamentals needed in the new situation.

Once I had the experience of conducting a large clinic. Sheets of drills were gone as soon as the stack of papers was placed on the table. The coaches wanted the answers. They wanted to be told the specifics of how to do their job. Teachers want this too. *No one can tell you how to best do your job*. It has to come from within. The magnitude of your experience and the accompanying resourcefulness is the path to sorting out the right material. A drill is something that originates out of trying to improve a fundamental. Fundamentals may be a combination of skills or movement patterns that enhance a specific athletic endeavor. The coach has to be able to isolate the raw component, then he will find ways to emphasize it with the athletes.

Recall the master coaches that sorted out the right material.

Recall good coaches that were lacking in this respect.

THE COACH IS LUCKY

The classroom teacher may not be able to communicate with every student each day, but the coach can. He works with every youngster from *all* backgrounds, all different personalities, all different abilities, and all enthused to make the strongest possible group. When the athlete gets overtired, the coach also has a chance to observe him in a less favorable light. Athletes are usually very hard working, naturally submitted to discipline, and seeking true objectivity. They place the group cause above personal gain, must be communicative, and must always be in the positive. The classroom just cannot compete.

What happens when the athlete leaves sports? There may well be a very positive correlation between the athlete's "play" patterns and his "work" patterns later on. I like to think there has been a lot learned that will carry over. But you cannot predict his performance on work he does not like. You are, however, in the best position in the school to write a character reference. The relationship is intimate. You know him "inside and out." Much of this has been alluded to, but you are lucky.

As a coach, I am sure you have been called upon to write character references on your athletes. What are some aspects the coach can evaluate that no other person can?

A COACH'S ROLE DURING A CONTEST

The coach has to see that the contest plan is carried out, with whatever adjustments needed, as well as possible. He is responsible for morale and getting the athletes to have their best performances.

One of your jobs that often comes home hard and fast is when a close contest is not going the way you want. You may be losing close races on judgment calls. You may be getting hurt in any sport by judgment calls. The coach's role has to be the right role.

One can get on the refs and so will the squad — a sorry sight. The coach can orient the group right on the spot so that their minds are on winning and doing their best and not alibiing for some past call. The official may be doing a poor job but you should get to that after the contest or during a time out when the squad is not affected. There are times, for other reasons, when one may do otherwise. However, it is easy to lose respect for the coach who loses his cool or gets on a ref to arouse his troops. You can win by being gentlemen. Good guys can win just as easily. It is more satisfying. If you do question the officials, it is better because of rule interpretation or something you are definitely right about. Questioning judgment could be almost everywhere and something to be avoided during most contests. Take the right approach and you gain strength all around. You lose if you try to question and lose the point. Your athletes should believe that you will fight for their rights, and then when you do it, you will choose the right time and you will win. This concept needs to be conveyed to them — this is good coaching. Good judgment avoids a lot of problems for your team and for you and strengthens you as coach.

One team could have bad breaks, the other could think they have bad breaks. Whatever the case, decide which way you want your squad to react. A team can go away feeling cheated and react very unfavorably in the locker room or on the field, and it all could be avoided by the perceptive coach that knows how to look at a contest and just when to act on deviant behavior.

Many times the coach is exposed to potentially explosive situations. It is very satisfying to see your athletes get on top of it all and come through acting in such a way that you feel proud to be associated with them. As a coach, you could have experienced embarrassment by lack of action or the wrong action. You will have many chances to come through a winner in this department.

Think of the many many times you have observed both positive and negative coaching behavior.

ONE OF THE ARTS OF COACHING

The successful coach has to sort out important beliefs and have his group think as much alike as possible. He needs to gain their dedication concerning his most vital issues. The development of discipline toward these issues has to always be enhanced. His job is to place as much discipline on his athletes as he feels they are able to accept. How much he can ask depends on his athletes and their past backgrounds. It also depends on the situation. Some situations have youngsters with or without the proper habits of discipline. Other combinations are limited by the academic, social, and traditional settings. Regardless of the variables that dictate the extent of imposed discipline, the goal of every coach is to get as much discipline as can be enjoyably accepted by the athletes.

Record your observations of coaches that missed and the coaches that seized on the opportunity to gain just a bit more discipline. This is a topic of special emphasis.

THE AMBITIOUS COACH DOES NOT MISS ON THIS ART

When the athletes take to the field, pool, court, or whatever their environment, their actions in warm-up and practice are greatly influenced by how the coach approaches the day's work. In some sports during pregame, it is easy to get involved with a small group or with an individual, a team member, an opposing coach, or a parent or friend for more than a very brief period of time. Team members may feel that they are being neglected. The coach must always observe and give the appearance of seeing every move that every person is making. He must convey the attitude he wants for that contest. They will prepare for the contest better if he is conveying the mood, watching everything that is happening, and making comments. If he is giving the appearance of being preoccupied at any time, he can lose their giving a little extra for him. He also gains respect when he is the overseer of it all. A coach must be teaching almost all of the time, or at least preparing to, by watching them closely. If he lets a warm-up or a drill that is being done sloppily continue that way, then he is asking for more of the same later on. The sharp coach is looking and guiding all of the time he is with his athletes. When the athletes are at the pool, court, or field, you are the one that is focal to all that happens. You convey the atmosphere. Set the stage.

How often have you observed coaches letting this important moment slip by?

PERSISTENCE

Success, for the coach and athlete, is 95 percent persistence. Records are set by talented individuals and broken by determined athletes of lesser ability. A phrase often quoted that we used on the board was originated by Admiral Hayward. "Nothing in the world can take the place of persistence. Talent will not. Nothing is more common than unsuccessful men with talent. Genius will not. Unrewarded genius is almost a proverb. Education alone will not. The world is full of educated derelicts. Persistence and common sense are omnipotent. The slogan — press on — has solved and always will solve the problems of the human race." I believe that, and I believe that the successful coach is the one who persists with his beliefs.

It is embarrassing to have an athlete who just didn't develop for you and later on becomes, for example, a fine marathon runner. Of course there are all kinds of reasons, but it can make a coach think. He became more dedicated after leaving your program. Persistence has to be in each day, each year, and years. Get the athlete to believe early on and good things will happen much faster. Goal setting, physical conditioning, success-failure patterns, and leadership are all interrelated. The coach is vital to all of these factors.

The top-notch coach brings home this point. Do you know of any coaches that emphasized this? Coaches that missed on some of their athletes?

A CAUTION TO COACHES

A high school athlete may experience too much practice. He may not want to take on a later commitment in college. Once set free from his past environment, it is easy to not want to dedicate to that same extent again. The great ones can do it and like it. It is sad, however, to see an athlete, like an experienced diver, with ten or more years of work behind him, just get enough of it by the time he attends college. He could be on his way to greatness. A high school athlete can, so to speak, get burned out, or lose his mental edge, if worked too hard. *Enjoyment* must be an important part, and the good coach knows when to ask only what is appropriate for time and place. I would not want to be a coach, no matter how successful, if my athletes did not want to continue on afterwards. Do not confuse the issue. An athlete from a good program is disciplined, hard working, can handle outside problems, and is great for the college coach to have. However, there is a *limit* to what a coach should ask of some youngsters. Fun is your guide — all kinds of hard work and discipline are good if he likes being in the program. It's up to you to be aware of the long-term effects. Don't be afraid to make it less competitive within the squad and in your competition. If each day the athletes are enjoying everything they do, they will work hard for totally intrinsic reasons — a good motivational source. Even the coach can work so many hours that he will wake up some morning and want to do something else.

Have you seen athletes from both settings? Experienced "burned out" athletes? For your sport, time, and place, what would you ask of your high school athlete?

Be as articulate for your sport, time, and place regarding the college athlete.

A GREAT COACH AND A GREAT ATHLETE

One of the plus points of the American system of athletics is that we often have a very close athlete to coach relationship. Other countries may have a special physiologist, kinesiologist, trainer, and special M.D.'s to supervise diet, sleep, etc., but most important of all is the mental relationship that exists between a coach and athlete. This writer believes that more can be accomplished with the coach and athlete working closely together than through exposure to more specialized knowledge.

The athlete must be in a competitive and mentally comfortable environment. The athlete also needs a one-to-one coach intimacy to get the best performance. I think we can agree that to go all the way to the top alone is very difficult.

A great athlete may be quite self-directed or may be wanting all practice details outlined for him. The self-directed athlete goes a long way, as he strongly believes all he does is right. Even if it is not the right thing needed, it is practiced extra hard. Self-reliance is enhanced and counts a lot, but unless he is open, he may not reach his ultimate. Equally successful can be the athlete that relies very heavily on everything his coach outlines for him. In fact, if he is equally dedicated, he may experience other advantages. One advantage is to possibly benefit from the coach's experience. At competition time, he is more subject to doing what the experienced coach conveys in order to be successful. The totally self-directed athlete is subject to making more costly mistakes.

Regardless of which type of athlete, there can be a mental breach for one reason or another between coach and athlete. Then a fine coach is unsuccessful, and a fine athlete is unsuccessful. The challenge is for this to be recognized and for the coach to be super aware of creating a comfortable and communicative atmosphere.

Whatever problems that must exist, be careful not to let any breach occur that does not have to occur. Confine your relationship breaches to your fundamental coaching philosophy. Be sensitive to out of practice endeavors so not to create a breach in what you and the athlete can accomplish. For special emphasis here, remember that a great coach and great athlete may not make it together. Both coach and athlete should recognize this. There should be no great guilt if both usually have successful relations with others. The challenge for the coach, however, is to have a 100 percent success rate.

Have you witnessed the specialized knowledge approach to coaching?

Have you experienced the close one-to-one psychological relationship?

Cite the many examples of each kind of athlete and how the coach fits in.

Analyze the cases you are familiar with and try to determine the factors why the outstanding coach and athlete may not have been able to make it together.

WHAT KIND OF TEACHING?

We have stressed the teaching of good technique. We have also emphasized that the basic human qualities can easily be taught. The leader can teach many things by *example*. *Good human qualities displayed by the coach get results.*

Cheerfulness permeates others. Basically, kids like to joke and have fun, and you should too. However, you are never wrong to keep your comments related to business with a fun comment that lets them identify you.

Common sense is another cherished quality and one of the most lacking in the school setting. In fact, this is a value problem of the world. Your daily approach can go a long way in helping others.

If you reason well and explain why to do things a certain way, it teaches basic decision-making by example.

If you are quick on the trigger and not always right, you can expect your athletes to display some of the same. It is amazing how many will act through your kind of thinking. *Emotional stability* is a must.

If you are kind and cooperate easily with whatever is needed to be done, you also teach *service to others,* for example, to give an out of town ride that some youngster really did not need when you really did not have the time may ensure his doing the same for others someday.

Unselfishness of time, sympathy, sharing, and displaying loyalty are all qualities that you can promote, largely by possessing these in your daily life.

If one asks, what is education, and if you want to defend the above qualities, you have a very strong case. Classroom related? Certainly. These qualities, however, can easily be in the forefront of every sports season.

How many kinds of teaching does this bring to mind?

Do you feel you can be a good teacher by example?

OTHER KINDS OF TEACHING

The day-to-day job of working with your athletes centers around your ability to make them perform better. This involves detailed teaching of techniques. How to change a technique has already been emphasized. A key phase is *"assume that they know nothing."* This means that basic information has to be repeated many times as the athlete is not always mentally ready to learn what you want. You may have not made it clear with aids. If you did do a great teaching job, it may have meant different things to different people. Even if the athlete gets the message and knows what you want, he may not be able to do it. A typical example is as follows: You teach a simple basic skill many, many times to the athlete and "assume" he understands. After a year or two of constant reemphasis on your part, he may come to you with a sharing of *his* discovery of what you had told him. It could be his repeating your exact phrase like he never heard you say it at all — sort of learned it somewhere by osmosis or whatever. That's the way it goes. Thus, being overly basic in teaching the fundamentals is vital.

Apart from basic teaching, the athlete also is in great need of constant orientation. They have to be alert to many things such as which contests they must peak for and just when they will come. Your most experienced athlete will oftentimes be preoccupied with a girl, studies, or whatever and will surprise you at being disoriented. It is imperative that all, including your most experienced, be right on target for each day, the week's work, and performance.

Teach the habits of *healthful living.* Youngsters learn by doing and by good environmental examples.

Learning leadership and followship roles by sorting out the importance of each. This is *appreciation by participation.*

Perhaps most important is the learning of *loyalty,* often found directly proportional to what each gives of himself. We stressed this in our last topic from the point of view of a coach's example.

A great deal of learning has to be simple — *habit formation and basic patterns and choices* added to *memory.*

Count the many mistakes coaches have made because they "assumed." Record the endless orientation errors.

You can also add to the many "other kinds of teaching."

ANOTHER JOB

The coach wants to win, but winning at all costs is not part of it. How does the coach that allowed a pitcher to throw the first pitch and then protests the game for his being used fit in? Not the best way to handle a question. It is dwelling in a negative. Much better is it to bring your concern in the open at the proper time for the good of the athlete, the contest, and for sport.

If you as coach have put into the game in preparation and administration all that you have, then live with the outcome. If the athlete has done his best that he was capable of that day, then he can rest. If losing involves either parties not having that feeling of their having been into it with every stone unturned in preparation and every ounce of effort, they have much to think about. Regardless, *to the winner of a well-balanced and played contest goes an elation as very few feelings in this world, and to the loser goes a sober rededication and waiting for the next day to begin again.* The coach knows of these feelings in the life of sport, and his job is to be sure his charges have given their all, and after sportsmanlike acceptance of the win or defeat, he sums up the contest with his athletes so that they will have the proper learning experience with their efforts. It is what you've worked so hard for. The coach must use his experience, channel the innate enthusiasm of what happened, and create the mental setting for the coming preparation.

Have you known coaches that could not accept defeat properly?

How many coaches have you observed that did not live by a philosophy of being a fine competitor and gentleman?

FACTORS LIMITING SUCCESS

Equipment and facilities can be a limiting factor.

Budget limitations, thereby cutting rosters of team members who can travel, is another example of restrictions on success. Finances alone can be such a problem of the present and future that they place otherwise fine programs on an intramural basis.

Just as good facilities attract, poor facilities can hurt. However, it is still possible to find excellent programs where inferior facilities exist. But environment does make a difference.

Administrative attitudes are often another negative. The coach oftentimes has to cover and be enthused. You are lost if you blame the administration. The attitude is negative and it permeates. You are also disloyal. This is a challenge.

The competition and number of contests are other limitations.

The locality can be even another problem. It is more difficult to produce top-notch swimming or baseball teams in the north country when you cannot get outside as much of the year and enjoy the outdoor competition.

You as a leader are the one, the most important factor in program success. Outstanding programs very often relate directly to one person's efforts — the coach. Just about everyone has limitations so you will have a lot of company.

What other limitations have you experienced?

Make note of some coaches who were successful regardless of limitations.

Chapter 7

BETTER UNDERSTANDING
THE ATHLETE

THE ATHLETE DEFINED

T HE word "athlete" is often misused. The common misuse of the term "athlete" is when one is evaluated on physical ability alone. To observe raw ability or performance without some essential ingredients is very shallow.

An athlete has a code of personal behavior that enhances performance goals. We all have had many participants that had excellent raw talent, but those select few that often had lesser ability will always remain in mind as the real athletes.

The outstanding "performer" may not train and may not have any worthy behavior habits. He may have good performances, but if he does not train properly, there are three ingredients lacking. He will not be consistent in a highly competitive situation. Second, he certainly cannot be performing near his level of potential. It seems difficult to honor efforts that are less than the best. The third lacking quality — he is not mentally helping others on his team if in no other way by his example alone. Any experienced coach knows that the athlete that gives mentally to every other person on the squad makes a *more important* contribution to the ultimate goals for success than mere physical performance. If the outstanding "performer" does not add a mental contribution, he is taking away by creating a less than expected example.

There are many athletes who have great dedication to sport and all that has to be mastered. They have a fine code of personal behavior that enhances goals. They have an unwavering single-mindedness for accomplishment and excellence. They have a fine mental and emotional desire as expressed by long-term intellectual commitment. The ultimate athlete goes a step further and is a person with a balance of pride and humility and with class in his actions. He is held in high esteem by all who know him. Physical ability, as other characteristics, is just a part of the true athlete. To honor the "outstanding athlete" is to honor a much larger and more meaningful package than just physical performance.

Have you experienced the misuse of the term "outstanding athlete?"

What is your definition of "outstanding athlete?"

When awards for "outstanding athlete" are being made, how should they be introduced? Draw up your criteria.

Would it be more appropriate to call the award "the most valuable" as selected by fellow teammates?

Should a team sport not have awards?

THE COACH CAN BE SURPRISED

I have had youngsters reach heights that I didn't believe they could attain, which is a sad portrait of a coach. About anything is possible with a human being, and the coach should expect great things. Have you ever underestimated potential?

This topic is worthy of note, as the coach should be the dreamer and leader of goals as to what the athlete can accomplish. Never should the coach feel the embarrassment of having his athlete perform well beyond the horizons of what he estimated that athlete could do. Experience helps the coach be on top of "potential."

Young men often believe that they can do anything if they put their minds to it. They are quite often close to being right. You, as their coach, should believe that your kids are as good as any others you meet, they are just in different stages of physical and mental development. You have to provide them with good competition, successful challenges, and the reevaluation of goals that continually change as one hits new plateaus. Constantly encourage, work on mental coaching, be the leader in setting goals, and show them the way. The reason this topic is covered is that it is commonplace to observe a coach joking about the lack of his talent or not conveying great belief in his athletes.

The coach that misses in estimating a youngster's potential is embarrassed. It's like being outcoached. It is analogous to a coach getting just a play behind. There are games that go that way. As you may know, once you get a little behind in the contest, it is very difficult to get back on top again. Y. A. Tittle said it best when he stated, "that once you lose the whip you seldom ever get it back." Perhaps prior preparation could have been the cause.

At any rate, the successful ingredient is the *day-to-day* preparation that goes into making an athlete go that extra mile. The coach has the vital role. Coach Julian, former Dartmouth College basketball coach, once said at an athletic banquet, "you are only as successful as your organization." This means the coach and the other players have to be successful, too, in order for any one athlete to be as outstanding as he aspires. This implies to me that a cooperative venture as being the best avenue to success. The coach and the athletes have to dream of the top together — you as leader.

Have you experienced the coach downgrading his talent?

How many athletes have you witnessed go beyond what the coach predicted?

A SPECIAL RESPECT FOR THE ATHLETE

We all have observed the coach that is constantly berating his athletes from the sideline. Perhaps he is at a loss for something more important to do. Perhaps he is getting after his athletes for making mistakes that he should have been working on earlier in preparation. Perhaps he is making a couple of other mistakes as well. For sure, he is not coaching to win. He is also in the negative, a poor posture for operation, and the kids are thinking negative — like blaming the officials and not thinking about getting things together. This point is emphasized, after being mentioned twice before, because it is such a common coaching mistake. This aspect also relates to many other issues.

Respect has to be a vital part of all your dealings. If the coach shows respect for his athletes, he will observe this quality in their dealings with others. *The athlete in last position must also have the respect* and support of the coach and the rest of the squad. All athletes are there to learn and to do what they can in competition. The coach that takes a view that here is an athlete — never a poor one – that is only at a different stage of development, is looking at things properly. The coach should enjoy teaching this youngster because he wants to learn. This is a fundamental concept. It is emphasized here because of the way some coaches treat their third or fourth string members. If ever there is a reference to inferior status by anyone whatsoever, such as from other squad members, it must be dealt with on the spot. Terms like the "hamburger squad" or "rag nots" must never be used. There should be only praise for every member's efforts. Over the years, the most lasting contributors have often been the athlete who had a supporting role. They had the toughest role by far – never a front-runner. These athletes are often the longest remembered for all they did. It takes a lot more to fulfill that role than to be in the limelight. When the season is over, that person has to have a special place in the coach's heart.

Make note of the instances of respect and disrespect you have experienced.

Also list the cases of third and fourth stringers that were the real winners.

THE AVERAGE ATHLETE

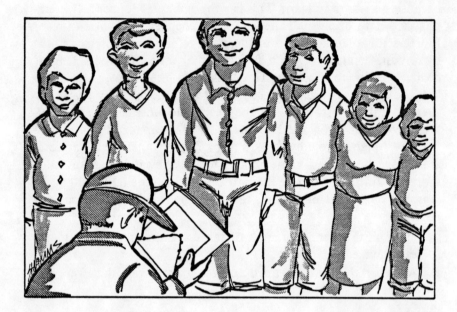

In an attempt to clarify an overview of an average team, let's try to categorize the typical squad. We all know what the elite 15 percent is like. They are "winners." They score when you need it most. They are consistent, well prepared, and tough, the blue chippers.

The other end of the spectrum is the lower 15 percent. They are there. They don't seem to be like the blue chippers in coming through. In fact, they have their best days when you are already winning and no pressure is on. Some call them front-runners. But it is really just a youngster who has not arrived — most of these youngsters never will. Some of them are there for friendship. They may not realize that friendship is achieved only out of respect for what they do. Some like the prestige of the organization. If the sport is prestigious, then it attracts. Others want to get in shape. Others have goals that are not clear and often are unrealistic.

The average athlete, the middle 70 percent, is the in-between. This group should include the lower 15 percent we described, because many can be shown the way to win. Almost all have a strong reason for being out for the squad. Goals must be made a bit more clear and realistic. They are there and want to get better. They are volunteers and this is a step in the right direction.

The coach's job is to try to make each athlete come along as fast as he can. He has to provide confidence situations in daily practice and contests so that the athlete can experience success. He has to develop good work habits, good conditioning, greater desire, confidence, and intensity in all he does. The average athlete needs a special emphasis on success situations if he is to become a "believer" as soon as possible.

The above analysis is like bringing a fighter along. He learns in a positive way. He must be challenged each time out, but he must have success rather than receiving the knock-out punch. After a while, he believes. He is confident in what he does. He is in the right frame of mind for success. So it is true with other sports. The coach must see that especially the average athlete is brought along right. To make winners or to have a greater percentage of winners from all categories is your goal.

Do you know coaches who already categorize their potential? How many have you seen come along later and defy the categories — despite the coach?

What are some specific things a coach can do to bring the average athlete along in your sport?

HE MUST BE APPRISED OF THIS

An athlete, as part of his practice preparation, has to under-stand that he will have good days and bad days. Many things in preparation help the athlete have fewer bad days. He must be pre-pared to deal with defeat. You cannot prepare for each individual setback. Thus, some special awareness by the coach can pay great dividends.

My son once struck out in the last inning of an important game. A thinking and perceptive coach saw that he was taking it hard and said, "One thing about baseball, there is always another day soon." This kind word made life fit together again. The ath-lete has a great need for the coach's approval. Be prepared for the inevitable setbacks and be positive. Some you can help ahead of time, some you cannot.

How does goal setting help? How could it even detract?

What are some ways the alert coach can help the athlete?

THE DAY-TO-DAY WORK INVOLVED

We have emphasized that the coach's legacy is hard work. We have emphasized the great need for hardworking leadership to create hardworking athletes. Perhaps you as an athlete or as a coach have been very successful without hard work. I have gone through seasons where we were very successful win-loss wise, but I knew that year's effort was not my best. Beware, as sooner or later you'll come to believe in the work ethic for sure.

The athlete learns before his participation days are over that his legacy, too, is hard work. He holds a special position by his output. Respect goes to the worker. Lack of respect goes to the loafer. They all know.

The coach not only by example but by his guidance must get across to the athletes that here is the place for "work." All else is extra. Athletes want to work hard. The saddest of all comments to the coach is when an athlete can say, "We should work harder." They want to be pushed. You, as coach, can let up after a practice that is too tough, but you may never really know where you are at if your work is on the light side.

Have you seen squads that are not hardworking? What is their conditioning level? Are they mentally tough?

What are many of the side benefits of extra hard work?

AN ATHLETE'S NEED—A COACH'S NEED

If both the athlete and coach have a good relationship and can adjust to each other so that communication is on high level, they probably had to make some compromises along the line. Flexibility, as emphasized earlier, is very necessary.

A past and classic issue was long hair. Some coaches said that if you cut your hair to my specifications, I will accept you and do what I can for you. It was a logical request in many ways. The coach was responsible for team image. When they travel, outsiders inquire about the group. Many older citizens tag a whole team by the dress or appearance of a few. The coach believes that to play well, you have to dress well. You have to think positively, and it will rub off. This is traditional and quite right as far as it goes. But there certainly can be a youngster that works harder than the rest and yet does not want to conform. What, then, does the coach do? Lose the athlete and perhaps the squad, or does he accept most things and let the rest be forgotten?

I was once caught up with this issue. One of the hardest workers I ever had taught me a lesson. He was very biochemically efficient and could handle nearly double the work of his teammates. He had long hair. I talked to him about it. He had left school and been gone a few years. It happened that he was in the Marine Corps and had been in Vietnam for a couple of tours of duty. He said, "Coach, I've had my discipline, and I'll give you all the work you can hand out and do all you want me to, living habits and all; however, I want to dress as I see fit." A couple of days later his picture came out as a full page in the local paper. He was shown as an example of "the best dressed man." Luckily, I had already resolved my conflict. I had indicated to him that I thought he was right. Before that time, I had made mistakes. From the day I honestly dealt with it, I never saw hair after that. If the athletes could accept my short hair, I could accept their long hair. They had already accepted me.

How about the athlete in a sport like track or swimming who sometimes wants to do a certain workout but it is not yours. You don't feel it is the best for him, but you realize that if he likes it, it will be done extra hard and probably yield about the same results. As long as you don't lose him to his own each day and he works close with you in planning, why not make one adjustment for the boy who wants to work hard and believes in what he is doing. That is *flexibility*. He should see you a day ahead of time so that you can review his request and include your goals too. You are the master. Keep that spot, but give a little. The coach can have the philosophy that "I'll do all the thinking, you generate the hard work." This is a clear-cut relationship, but is more accomplished? Are thinking athletes developed? The top echelon of athlete is often quite a strong, thinking, and creative person.

The issues are many but they are crucial ones oftentimes, and it takes communication and both sides working for a common goal for compromise to occur, and then you have flexibility. If both goals are established and are being met, what makes the difference how they are met?

Can the coach be flexible and still be strong? Build your case for each side.

Cite examples of athletes and coaches losing out because of not compromising.

RECOGNIZING SPECIAL NEEDS OF THE ATHLETE

One of the needs that most all athletes have is the need to be close to the coach, to identify, and to converse. Some are very obvious in that they choose to call you by your first name—almost too soon it seems. But this is a cue that perhaps there was a special need.

Go along and be available when the athlete wants to spend some time and talk. Having time for students is a must. Coming to work extra early while the day is quiet is when most of the day's work gets done. The early hours are the productive ones. After early morning and after a couple of hours of steady, uninterrupted work, look for students to talk to and always try to have some time when they want to see you.

Another youngster with special needs is often a manager who wants to be where the others are. He often has the need to be especially close and accepted even though he is not an athlete. Look at all the work he does to gain acceptance. Others, of course, are there for different reasons. I once saw one of my former managers after some twenty years. I had often thought of his need to be around and share part of his life with me. I had not given him as much as I would have liked. I was young and had not been very perceptive. I even let the squad kid him a bit, thinking it was fun for him too, until one day he went away in tears. I learned something about his needs and remembered with guilt for many years. It was nice to learn twenty years later that he did not remember the bad experiences. He remembered some really positive experiences that I did not recall. I had finally shed some guilt feelings and was relieved.

Some coaches believe that it is good to be aloof and not figured out by the athlete. Coaching out of fear? However, I believe there is a special need to be predictable. Being predictable is a sign of stability, sureness, maturity, and there is nothing wrong with the athlete knowing exactly what you are like. In fact, the more he knows about you, the more he can identify or feel you are a human being—identifying with both your strengths and weaknesses. You are also the benefactor when you get to know the athlete in every way. Then you can better work with him also.

A special and common need is the desire for success. Some have a tremendous need, and you have to be on top of every day and every meet to be sure he is responding in the right way. The older coach knows what some of the mistakes can be and shares these with the athlete beforehand so that more of his behavior is predictable.

Make note of all the special needs athletes may have—there are many, many more.

THE CONCENTRATED OPPORTUNITIES

The nature of a sports season is rushed. The goal is to win the race against the season's time. You have limited time to produce the best possible group strength. There are many things that happen in coaching that may not normally happen in other kinds of work. A youngster may approach you with a problem that seems gigantic to him. You get involved and help him through his crisis. This is your job, just another day. When an athlete gets injured and you may have to forget all other commitments and follow him through, it is just a part of your job of caring. But the opportunity is there for growing as a coach and as an athlete. When the youngster comes up to you the next day and makes it a point to thank you for helping him out, you know you have done something worthwhile for your extra hours spent with him.

Interpersonal Relationships

Perhaps the greatest day-to-day observance of life in concentration is the interrelationships between one athlete and the other. It is easy for two youngsters to be happy and get along when they are not tired and working hard. When they are physically drained, things get sticky. Here is a great teaching moment. You are able to discuss the value of positive thoughts. You bring home the need for encouraging words to other teammates. The athletes have to realize that there are trying times. One has to learn how to handle his true emotions. This is an important job for the coach.

Learning How to Win and Lose

Handling the winning and defeat is perhaps where the greatest opportunities exist. Tremendous elation and dejection often occur in sport, and the coach plays a vital role. Every individual is a unique being, and as such, he reacts in a different manner. The athlete has to be guided for proper behavior. Athletics without a good coach during crucial times is not necessarily intrinsically good. The coach's role in helping athletes learn to win and lose is crucial.

Intimate Dealings and Guidance

Generalizations are hard to make when dealing with athletes. The successful coach realizes that there is an art in using to advantage what you have learned about young people. Behavioral patterns vary tremendously, and the coach has to use great perception to create the proper setting for successfully dealing with the athlete.

Two young athletes may act in the same way about a problem, but it is your knowledge of how each other's life is different that makes your dealings truly meaningful. One may have a personal problem with his parents or girl friend while one may have a history of more success or more failure. One may have a stronger mental tenaciousness. Another may have school problems. Still another is not having the immediate success he wanted, thus not having a prestigious place among his teammates. The athletes do not have everything "together," and when you can find some of the ways to help, you become really effective in your relationship. Closeness that fosters guidance may be lacking in some sports where more people are involved.

A Coach May Have to Deal Successfully in This Setting

There are some college situations where scholarships are not given on need. Athletes are sort of purchased goods—almost professional. However, a coach can quite easily rationalize the partial scholarships and have the athlete believe it is for time lost from work during his year. He is helping an athlete with his values. Thus, one can see that life is indeed gray—not just black or white, and the coach has to fit his beliefs into the situation in which he is working. There is no attempt to answer this question, as there is no single answer to fit all situations one might experience. Some coaches may not find harmony with their beliefs and an institution's philosophy. Not many coaches could adjust to situations that are incompatible with their philosophy.

How many other problems and/or opportunities can you recall that arise from the concentrated life aspect of sport?

GETTING THE ATHLETES TO HAVE THEIR BEST PERFORMANCES

It is your job to totally orient him or her to all of the circumstances that will affect the outcome. For example, if a coach fails to discuss what can happen, shock can ruin the afternoon.

A fast two or three touchdowns can ruin the chances for a fine team if they were surprised. They were overwhelmed because they had not thought of this possibility. An upcoming game could have fast scoring. The coach should be sure that the squad understands that the coming game could have some fast or early scoring. He would indicate that if this occurs, the team will not be affected and they will win in the latter part of the game. It makes all the difference in the world. It is like being psyched in rather than being psyched out. It really does occur on all levels of competition. The experienced athlete is prepared, in the positive, for all happenings.

The coach who has prepared seems to be at peace. Try to out-coach your opponent during the week in preparation. If the die is cast right, then the coach is more relaxed, confident, and can be in more control during the contest. Thus, the athlete benefits again by the coach's orientation.

Preparation in each sport is quite different. Time frames, short-term psyche, or long-term psyche are factors. The difference in success or failure is in orientation and in teaching effectiveness. In sports like track and swimming, where an individual may have special, independent workouts, some of your greatest effort must go to the self-directed athlete. This athlete may do all of the things he needs to, to be able to be at his best. He cares. He trains, he dreams about his sport and his role. But he can also be the one who will not so readily listen to the coach. The coach must be alert for any kind of preparation that does not include everything the athlete should have. In "individual sports" this is common. The athlete has put a lot into what he is doing, and it particularly hurts when he does not achieve his expectations. You can help by being super sensitive to how he is preparing. He may be doing your workout to a "T" but if he is quite self-directed, you can be sure his mind is miles apart from the others.

The "average" athlete may lean heavily on the coach. Whatever the case, the coach and team win by the preparation given before competition and the effective orientation received by the athlete.

Make note of all the different roles you have witnessed where coaching related to getting the best performance.

PROBLEMS MUST BE HANDLED FAIRLY AND INDIVIDUALLY

Perhaps an athlete must be excused from practice early or even miss practice. Care must be given to explain this to all of the squad. You need to make mention of what the other athletes observe and explain why you let it happen. If you fail to openly discuss the situation, others will follow suit and want to have the privilege whether they need it or not.

Involving the squad in a discreet way in discipline matters informs them and helps them understand the rules in practice. They must know their limits. This is how they differentiate right from wrong. The rules as outlined earlier can become cloudy later on in the season. Untried rules and even misinterpretations by different individuals are potential problems.

Rules are needed for effective administration, and frequent orientation to them prevents hurting a youngster unnecessarily, and in turn, this helps the team and you as coach. It is important to avoid the crises oriented coaching situation. Any coach *will* have problems relating to discipline. The experienced coach often displays more wisdom.

List all of the various kinds of discipline problems and relate each to a hypothetical or real conclusion.

How can most discipline problems be avoided?

DEVELOPING INDIVIDUAL AND TEAM LEADERSHIP

The election of a captain is very important. It is a factor directly related to individual and team leadership. He helps you and he helps his teammates. In some sports, this role might not be so vital, but in most it is a vital concern. To have the most popular athlete elected may not provide any support for the coach or any leadership among his peers.

I have seen many different procedures that profoundly affected the outcome. Here are examples: Fraternities have banded together to elect *their* captain, when the real leader was outside of their living unit. A captain, seeking votes for his friend, influenced a lot of unthinking athletes just prior to the voting process. Another negative observation occurred when the coaches changed votes—a very risky and unethical process. The coaches did this to keep a youngster from leaving school when he had one more season of athletic eligibility. The thinking was that if he was captain he would return, and knowing how well he was needed, a close vote was changed. Another experience was to see cocaptains elected when the vote was actually not that close.

Election time change was another observation. The time was moved up so groups would not so likely be involved in prevoting politics. Another example is that publicity had been given to an athlete, and this hurt support others would have given this potential leader had the voting been earlier. A time change to a later date at the beginning of a season was chosen when a new coach was appointed. All election problems were no real fault of the athlete. A fault due greatly to the *lack of dignity given this event.*

One of the best ways to assure honesty, thought, and dignity to the process is to write out your idea of the role of captain in your sport. This helps the voter know what is expected. The rules should always be the same, however. If you have just one captain, then even in a year when you feel the senior leadership is not so good, it still should be given to him. Athletes can lose faith in the event when rules are changed. Athletes can gain faith in the election of their captain if the coach speaks to the seriousness, the requirements, and asks for their most private and heartfelt vote. Athletes grow and surprise everyone in tackling responsibility, so do not be surprised when an unlikely candidate is chosen and turns out successful.

If dual captains are elected, be leery of just one doing all of the work; this often is natural. Don't misunderstand, it is often good to have duals. If other than seniors are elected, there could be another potential problem. The risk is that when they become seniors they may not receive another vote of confidence, and this could deny the best for the squad and also demote a senior when he is potentially most capable. If an athlete is to mature to his best, it could well come in the last year. At any rate, it is an important function and must be quite consistently conducted. From my experience, I like one captain and prefer he be a senior. The experience of seeing a junior captain not being reelected, for whatever reason, hurts the individual—he had his reward as a junior. He is not in a good growth situation.

Let's assume you have a captain. The captain must be given his role, as each person is capable of leading in a different way. The coach must spend a lot of time with him and have him realize just how he can be their leader.

Leadership in another way: Be particularly concerned that your upper classmen supply the right kind of leadership to the younger athletes. Cultivate this group, because if they break training, you can be certain that you will have the younger ones do so, too. If your seniors realize their role and will be close and not apart from the freshmen and sophomores and if they will tolerate only proper behavior, team leadership is greatly enhanced. The coach must be aware of this faction and must meet specifically with them to create this vital atmosphere. Once discipline breaks down, it may take years to get a grasp on things again.

The support environment has a lot to do with what takes place. In some communities, sport is so important that everyone is in a supportive role—large crowds and the peer pressure is good. This is easy. But in some sports where the season is long, perhaps where the crowds are sparse, where the motivation is often individually based, and where the kind of athlete is from a background not supportive of your ideals and disciplinary goals, you have a special problem. To stay on top of student leadership is important. This is a factor that will affect your success. A great leader is "priceless." They don't come along very often. However, athlete leadership is key to your goals.

Make note of the various ways captains have been elected. What is your preference in a captain (single, dual, tri)?

What qualities do you like to see a captain possess?

What kinds of leadership from team members have you observed?

What are some things a coach can do to develop better individual or team leadership?

CREATING A CLOSE-KNIT GROUP

One of the most important elements for closeness and unity is time spent together. The concentrated life situation as well as the tremendous time involved makes for close friendships. If you can isolate your group, even greater ties between the athletes can be achieved. Preseason training camps achieve a great deal more than improved skills and conditioning. We know that the mental contribution is a most important asset. What better way to create unity, dependence, and dedication to the cause than to have the team together and share around the clock. The southern trip for colleges and some high schools is an example of a way of living together. If the coach handles people right and they have fun, but still keep their limits of discipline, they are close, and being close means they are working more toward sameness of goals and harnessing their people power—the most potent of all forces.

Having fund raising ventures is also a means of working together. Group identity enhances your goals. Fund raising also can alienate if the goals are not set by the athletes. Cookouts, hikes, and other group activities contribute to becoming close and working more as a unit.

Make note of all the pluses teams gain by spending extra time together.

What other ways have you noted squads spending extra time together?

VARSITY AND INTRAMURAL EMPHASIS

They are both volunteers that want to play, but the intensity varies with each group. The varsity athlete wants to excel, seek excellence, compete on a rigorous scale, and become his best. The intramural participant is seeking more fun than excellence. He may not want to practice two or three hours a day to get in super shape, polish skills, or build the most efficient team possible. He often wants to enjoy an afternoon and may even take on a commitment to join a team and meet regularly. There are many degrees just as there are on so-called "varsity" teams. The basic difference is recreation in leisure time rather than another hard and fast dedication.

Each program should be compatible with the other. Because limited facilities could be in great demand, the question could arise as to which should take precedence over the other. There is no pat answer. The intramural program may have many more participants in a given period of time. This may outweigh the varsity few having the playing area. However, one could experience having to give way to a segment of the varsity practice area and thereby not allowing some specialists to practice. This is acceptable at times, but what about when a youngster is playing around in the outfield having a cigarette? I could not help but make the parallel that it was a situation like denying the library to the top student wanting to do research in favor of a student going to the library to meet some friends. Most situations, however, have no conflict of this sort. Each program should complement the other.

Whatever your school's arrangement, most activities are vital to satisfying the needs of the student body and must be appreciated for what each is capable of doing. Lack of understanding causes gaps in communication. The coach has to understand and care about each program. For years, men and women did not understand what the other was trying to do and did not appreciate each other. Look at the women's programs now. Both groups are much closer to working with each other as a result of Title IX. It was long overdue and something that was right in most of what was asked, but why did it not take place naturally? It is not only lack of understanding but another reason is advanced that is very often a factor. The people on top, whether teams in a league or programs in a school, often control things. Many good leagues have broken up because of the teams at the top—and namely the coaches responsible—have had visions of taking their athletes further and have made their own rules or gone their own way. This often has not been for the good of the entire school program or the league. This is why good directorship is needed and why commissioners are employed for leagues.

Intramurals are fun, needed, important, and now can get many of the same values as from varsity sport depending on effort of student-athlete and the way the program is run. There should be no breach between varsity and intramurals. One program helps the other—either as a feeder for athletes or as a place for those not looking for a varsity commitment. Every situation has to be evaluated and related.

From your experiences, note the varsity and intramural programs that function well together. Have you noted those that were not compatible?

What rules could coaches and intramural directors make to enhance the goals of both programs?

THE GOLDEN MOMENT FOR THE ATHLETE AND THE COACH

Success. Winning can bring forth all of the hard work into great elation. There were times when the hurdles seemed insurmountable to you and the athletes, but they believed and they came out a winner—a winner over another well prepared team. The chills that go up your spine are worth every minute you put into your work. It makes you come back for more. The athlete experiences this, too, and it is your time to teach. They will believe easier than when you lose. However, after each contest, don't let the team trickle off without bringing them together and summing up the way the contest went and where you are going from that particular point. It is a teachable moment, and it makes them all focus together on whatever the coach points out as being important.

Especially for the experienced coach, there is more need and more to be said after a loss than after a win. At any rate, don't be one of the many that let special times pass you by without speaking out to your squad. This is what makes them identify with you. A team can die without this need being fulfilled. The experienced coach also enjoys this important part of his coaching job. It is when he comes forth and grows. It does not have to come only after a contest. It may follow any incident worth getting together about. Before a contest, the athletes need you even more. At half-time or throughout the event, you have to keep them all of singular thought and purpose. This is also a teachable moment. Distractions and frame of mind make this teaching more difficult. If you have doubts about distractions, wait until school begins and notice the fall off of learning at practice as compared to practices before classes began.

Another direct distraction is violation of the privacy of the locker room. When friends and fans can enter before the golden moment, you may lose on many accounts.

How many times have you noted athletes and teams being denied one of their most vital gatherings?

Recall your playing and/or coaching experiences and think of situations that have been used to yield great benefit to the athlete.

THE ATHLETE IS LUCKY

The athlete and coach are often very close. The athlete has a person in whom he can confide. He has a person that wants to help him and is ready to do so. If the coach can get special favors for his athletes, he will do athletics a disfavor. However, the coach is older, knows a lot of people around school and community, and can often help a youngster immeasurably through his contacts. The coach's role with the athlete is also enhanced because of this situation. The athlete is lucky to have such a relationship. He is lucky to have such an advocate.

How many ways were you helped by your coach?

PARENTS

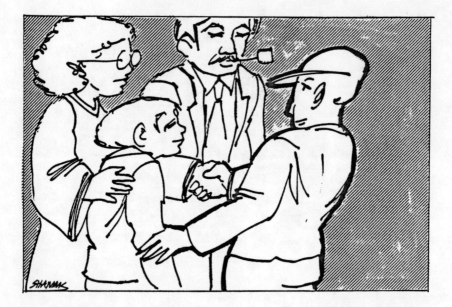

One of the best beginnings for athlete and coach is a proper supportive environment for the athlete—the ideal parent. This supporting parent helps his youngster enjoy play, his practice, and helps accept the sacrifices the child will have to make. This supportive parent understands that their child is in a worthwhile endeavor and needs their support. At times, their child will be tired, always in need of good nutrition, and in need of some help in getting to practice. If he is supported, he is developing loyalties to both the team and parents. He is free mentally because he knows that his parents approve of what is taking place. They want him to be good but accept his achievements. This is the ideal parent.

Another kind of parent has a negative feedback by words or deeds. I have known parents that disciplined their children by forbidding them to go to practice. I have seen others place a dependence on the youngster and prevent him or her from participating fully. The whole squad was hurt because the athlete could not participate. They were not supportive of his effort to himself or the team. His team responsibilities were minimized. This kind of situation could promote disloyalty in their child.

There are also overinterested parents. This is one example I experienced. The parent coached his child, pushed him hard, and even controlled all of his social life. Now his son was in college. His parents wanted to see him do his best swimming times. They had their watches on him and wanted personal success. They did not realize that their son was away from home for the first time in his life and had found other things important to him. He was not as dedicated as he had been. His social life and studies were consuming much of his efforts. They, in fact, had no idea of just what he had been doing. He was working quite hard, but the commitment he took on this year was not quite what it was in the past. He was free of some parental domination and enjoyed it thoroughly. He joined a fraternity and took on a lot of responsibility. His parents came to an important meet. The dad told his son just how to go about his race. The boy was obedient to his father and ignored the coach and did his best 500 time of the year on his way to a 1650 freestyle. But as expected, he tightened up because of going too fast. Before the race was over, his father stopped his watch and left the area in disgust over his son's performance.

This same youngster later in his career had some great times, but the success came when his parents did not attend. The times came when the coach got the most for the total situation. Domineering, overly interested parents do not make for the best combination for success. A coach must be on the lookout for such parental involvement and be sure that it is clearly understood that only one person can coach him at a time. These situations are hard for the young coach, and it is a fast way for the coach to mature.

The ideal parent should just want his child to *work hard* and have a *good attitude*. The ideal parent may also let the coach know he is available if there is anything that needs parental support. Just as there are x numbers of parents, there are x different ways that are involved.

List the many nonsupportive acts of parents.

How many parents do you remember that had the same goals as outlined? What are your goals?

What can you as coach do to promote the right parental support?

ATHLETES AS NORMAL HUMAN BEINGS

Giving Attention

Athletes, just like anyone else participating in any group endeavor, need to be appreciated for what is done. The athlete should leave practice feeling good about something. As a parent one year, I "rose" and "fell" with my son's feelings each day as he returned home from practice. Some evenings he was very discouraged after his hard efforts and sometimes quite elated. Some situations have minimal discouragement and others have a lot of it. What does a person, an athlete, do when he works hard and can't please? He does his share and forgets what is said. I prefer a coach that makes practice a place where guys like to come. They have to produce and work. It may well even be that the coach should not indulge in any laughter during his work period, but at least the coach should have a personal chat each day with each person or give each one some encouragement for doing something well. That's how you develop a positive attitude and that is how athletes feel good about themselves and, therefore, best develop.

Taking Words to Heart

Be sure you mean what you say. How many times have you heard a coach say, "That's good. Keep it up and you'll start Saturday." Or "You'll be playing a lot Saturday." The youngster works even harder and expects to get his chance and the coach forgets he ever said it. Saturday came and went and the athlete still did not get his chance. What happens? The youngster experiences a great letdown and from that time on does not really pay much attention to the praise of the coach. The athlete may even not hold him or the program in high esteem.

They Need Honesty

It is also not just trying to say good things. A coach may be a "goody-goody." Everything he says is praise. Praise is surely better than negativism as a steady diet, but when one really goofs, praise does little for the youngster. He needs honesty and to know what pleases and what does not.

The Athlete Wants to Please

Another ism that happens often is that a youngster works hard and does something quite well—say a technique that is being drilled. The coach says that's good—*"but"* and always says *"but."* In effect, the athlete cannot really please the coach. That too is discouraging.

The coach goes into his field to experience teaching through his sport and see young people grow. The coach, as well as the athlete, is seeking the experience of success and winning. You even develop the old hunting hound the same way. "Shared enthusiasm." It's basic. Sharing with the coach makes them real partners in doing. Win or lose, sharing is the right way—it is what it is all about, and you'll satisfy *all* the needs of athletes as normal beings.

Do you or did your coach make it a point to personally talk to you each day?

How many coaches do you know that are poor examples of what was emphasized?

A SUPPORT ENVIRONMENT

Just as parents can play a vital role in helping their children get involved and stay involved, booster groups and the community culture also play a great role in motivation. Youngsters want to be like their heroes. This is a potentially strong support environment and should be cultivated in whatever ways are possible.

What can the coach do to offer other support environments? He wants to make it appear that his program is the best. He wants to make it a place where all athletes want to be associated. Sometimes having large numbers is good. At other times a strong, small core of outstanding examples is better. The coach must decide.

A new coach often faces this problem: not wanting to work with mediocre seniors. It can lead to hard line cuts. The coach's major concern is creating ways to achieve the best possible discipline. However, sometimes cutting the seniors out is not the best way.

Contest publicity is a great help. Create school leaders. Make your own physical environment as much a work atmosphere as you can. You are responsible to create the best possible atmosphere, and there are many ways to do this. Bulletin boards and clean healthful areas to work also are a positive support environment. Any one aspect alone can be a great time consumer, but you have to do it or delegate it. It is important to delegate to keep up with the many opportunities to create better support environments, but you must keep under your direct control all things pertaining to your coaching atmosphere. Training camps, trips, outings, or gatherings, as previously mentioned, really create a support environment.

Teams that have pride want to identify as a group. It is common for the team to even come to you and ask to get T-shirts or other identifying wear. This is a sign that they are into it together. The alert coach emphasizes a support environment.

How many situations can you recall where there were poor support environments?

Could some of these environments have been changed by the thinking coach?

ATHLETES LIKE TO TALK AND MAKE SUGGESTIONS

Athletes like to converse. They like to make suggestions. An athlete who is thinking and contributing is a good one. A coach needs their input and has to foster this. Just as the coach can value an athlete's ideas on how things are going or what should be included in preparation, the coach can well use the athlete's conversation in other veins to help him tune the squad for their best effort. If you know a youngster "inside out," you are in a much better position to give the right prescription. Knowing each other intimately is a much better posture for all concerned. When athletes want to talk to you about practices, their work efforts, themselves, or whatever, you have a need to listen. The indication of intimacy is not disrespecting or hard for the truly self-confident and sensitive coach who knows his job. Only the unsure coach is leery of suggestion.

The coach just has to be the one to keep suggestions at exactly that level. Sometimes youngsters are not diplomatic. A young coach will possibly have trouble handling some kinds of input but as you become stronger, it becomes more valuable.

Have you noticed some coaches "cutting off" suggestions? How did it affect the athlete?

What could this coach have specifically done to bring out the athlete and still become stronger and a better coach himself?

ATHLETES ARE ALL DIFFERENT

Your job as a coach is to accept a youngster who has reported to you. You accept him, and through work, promote his confidence. You help him learn what his strengths are. But being successful in sport or in life is really taking your strengths and emphasizing them. Your job is to change him as much as you can to make him a valuable team contributor and a better person: but the "art of coaching" is to know when to lay off or not to try to change what the athlete does not want to change. This approach means that you not have great conflict with the athlete's personal values. Accept the athlete, help him find his strengths and weaknesses, change what you can, and forget about the rest. Some broad limits are a part of every coach's philosophy. This paragraph is somewhat repetitious to the "key job of the coach,"

but it needs emphasizing. The author has witnessed too many coaches that were out of contact and insensitive to what their athletes were thinking, and even more important, many coaches were out of contact in regards to what the athlete was like as a person. The coaches were either oblivious to the athlete's feelings and personal qualities or did not care. How can one coach properly without this bond of total acceptance? Just as athletes are all different, so are coaches. In effect, you are asking the athlete to totally accept you. Your total package should be appealing.

What can the coach do to actually promote individual differences and gain support and team unity as well?

THE ATHLETE NEEDS SPECIAL INGREDIENTS

The Right Competition

Without the right kind of degree of challenge, it is impossible to develop one's maximum. A low grade of competition will not bring the athlete along with challenges, and he may easily become self-satisfied and certainly not work at his level. If competition is too tough, no success is allowed and discouragement takes place.

A lower level of accomplishment can result in the end. The ideal situation is to have competition where the athlete is challenged enough to really press him and even cause his fundamentals to break down but to win or win a fair share of the time. Contact sports often need a special sensitivity to bring the athlete along. To allow a freshman to have physical contact, such as in a one-on-one blocking drill with an outstanding senior, can be devastating to confidence.

Fundamentals in an Enjoyable Way

The next ingredient that is needed is the stressing of fundamentals by repetition in an interesting way in practice. There are many, many fundamentals, and they have to be overlearned to stay with the participant during competition. A fundamental can be a specific skill, movement, or a part of a skill. Whatever is needed most should be repeated. The coach's job is to study his group and individuals and *come up with ways to repeat necessary fundamentals*. The whole-part-whole method of learning can make the fundamentals interesting. By understanding the whole picture through some play, the need and motivation is there for returning to the "parts" or fundamentals. Learning will take place with enthusiasm and at a faster rate than when the athlete is not sure of "why" the fundamentals and is sort of bored.

Super Conditioning

Aside from competition and specific fundamentals, the athlete needs another raw component—*conditioning that is superior during and after the season*. In any even contest, the superior conditioned athlete makes fewer mistakes and maintains pressure, which causes mistakes by their opponents.

Can you add more specialized ingredients?

KNOW WHAT EXCELLENCE REALLY IS

The basic issue is to seek excellence. A lot of youngsters work and think that they are doing quality work when in fact they are doing a mediocre job. Their progress is limited and they do not realize it. Your job is to get each player to know *what* an excellent job of practicing is and then to *do it*. There are really two issues—*the athlete knowing what is first rate performance, and second, he has to be able to make himself work at that intensity*. Some can, some can't.

The next step is to carry this idea to a team picture—constant orientation is needed so that they know the many ways to develop pride in all that they do. Each person has to see the value of his being at his best in a way that makes the team become its best.

I used to minimize mistakes and say that the game is full of them. Don't worry, just persist, and do as you have been coached to do. I did not want to have a hesitating athlete—one holding back because of the fear of making a mistake. This is a mediocre thought to plant in a young athlete's mind. On the other hand, to be unforgiving or to put too much pressure to bear on an athlete for mistakes can be equally detracting. The best posture is to have the athlete believe that the team that makes the fewest mistakes wins. The trick is to *be so well prepared that the mind is relatively free and the athlete automatically performs.*

Have you observed athletes who want to be exceptional but *do not really* know what excellent output actually is?

Have you observed coaches living by the next-to-last sentence but not the last sentence of this topic?

THE ATHLETE GROWS WITH RESPONSIBILITY

It is amazing how a coach often observes mediocre talent emerge into a fine leadership. It happens when responsibility is placed on youngsters. Upperclassmen and elected captains often mature to their needed roles. This aspect has been emphasized. However, guidance in letting the athlete understand his needed role is sometimes all that is required to get a change in capability to take place.

Some youngsters are "helpless" through much of their early lives, while some youngsters are "self-sufficient." This is true with your athletes and even adults. Give them the chance to lead, create a mold for them to live up to, be heard, and take part or they may not emerge with their talents in time to help themselves and the team.

Outlining goals off-season with each athlete is a great help to foster *personal responsibility*. During a season, the coach can be alert to whatever he can do to have each gain a more *personal responsibility* for his success and that of the team.

Categorize your squad. How many fall into the self-sufficient and responsible category and how many do not? What seems to be your ratio? It should tell you a lot about your group.

What are some things you can do to foster personal growth and responsibility?

Develop responsibilities for your captain that fit your sport.

WHAT MAKES A TEAM?

A team is made up of athletes and interesting factors. A team has characters and is of character. Let's take a look at "character." Character makes a team dig down and work for the outlined goals. Personality is a more superficial expression and is observed in day-to-day relationships. It rises and falls on sleep, hard work, and other variables. Character is something that one has developed by past experiences. It is part of innate makeup. It is like the "weathering well" over a long period of time. It is the ability to see what has to be done and then doing it. Some teams that just cannot give enough of themselves may not know how, while others can reach down deep and come up with the extra work to get the results they wanted. Character.

Do you teach character? In some ways, yes, and in many ways, you cannot. Past experiences occur over a greater time span and they may be more deeply engrained. Family ties, close relationships, work experiences, etc., all are a part of the environment. It's nice to find a team with a lot of what is needed—already there.

What are the many ways in which a sports season and a good coach can enhance the "degree" of character?

AN UNDEFINABLE THAT IS DISTINGUISHING

Everyone looks up to the athlete and team that has "class." For sure, no one looks up to "crude" athlete or team behavior. What is class? "Class" is doing the right thing at the right time. It is being polite, always a gentleman. It is using the right language, never being crude. It is friendliness to your own team and to those of other teams, as well as to others connnected with the program. Class is a steady predictable positive way of doing all that you do. "Class" seems to be the best word.

All coaches want this for their teams. It has to start with the actions of the coach and how he gets his goals across. From my experience, things like the above just don't happen without the proper leadership. It is hard to set down a hard and fast formula. It must be a sought out need, proper examples set, and then rewarded. Every squad is vastly different, and every coaching situation is also quite different, but a coach is successful if he can get youngsters to display "class."

It is a good exercise to set forth some examples of how the coach can get any squad to have "class."

AN ATHLETE CAN'T BE GREAT ALONE

Support environments have been emphasized, but a special emphasis has to be given to the coach's role in success. It is possible for a youngster to be outstanding by working alone. It is more difficult, however, to reach full potential. He must be challenged in just the right manner. This is even more noticeable when applied to a team. There are too many variables. Very few athletes will display the same effort as if another is alongside and pushing. The athlete that works alone is at a disadvantage. In some sports, it is common to see those doing work on their own. The odds are greater for success if the athletes and even more so the team are brought along at just the right way—asked to do more. We have all heard of the word "choke." Well, this is from lack of experiencing adequate challenges. An athlete that is well seasoned in tough competition is mentally and physically on top of what is needed to do his best. He has been asked to do his best enough times in tough situations that this is taken in stride. Everything is relative, but it is common to find successful Olympians that in their first time around just didn't have enough of that special preparation, and they did poorly. The next time around, the preparation was in the bank, and they did their best when they had to. It takes more time when exact guidance is not a part of their preparation.

The coach gets the right competitive situation, he motivates and creates confidence, and he establishes the right kind of relationship with his athletes so that they are attached and working together. The one-to-one relationship is the key and more important than the precise workouts given or the knowledge of kinesiology, physiology, or psychology. It is security and support, and more than that, it is leadership. A horse needs a master for good performance and so does a human need others, especially a knowledgeable coach. It is just plain hard to get as much done and prepared for the top alone.

Have the "loners" been as good as they could have been? How can the coach create less "I" and more "we?"

RECOGNITION

The right kind of publicity is a great help to your program—namely through the motivation of individual athletes. There is great need to see that each athlete has some recognition. I have seen youngsters hurt for the season in a sport because their names were left out of newspaper articles when others on the squad were mentioned. The situation may have been caused by an oversight due to the busy routine of the coach. An athlete's efforts that are not given recognition can cut down on his motivation. With the advent of Title IX and the doubling of the number of sports programs, the publicity in many local papers has been cut to nearly nothing. This has hurt those programs and individuals. The coach now has to work harder.

The coach may well invest some of this time in having pictures taken, placed on bulletin boards, and if necessary, doing some of the articles himself. He may be almost totally responsible for promoting this aspect. Giving praise is key. It is a problem for some coaches, but it is nevertheless a motivating factor that needs to be dealt with for this reason alone.

As an athlete or as a coach, what are your experiences?

List the specific benefits of recognition.

List the possible harm that you have observed from recognition.

THE PROBLEM ATHLETE

We have painted a positive picture of the athlete coming out for sport because he wanted to. It is assumed that he has enthusiasm and a fine attitude. This is pretty much the pattern. However, there may be those that want to be there—they could even be your most dedicated—but have a negative approach in dealings with others. When things do not go as expected or when that person is tired and overworked, relations are very strained. It is certainly a challenge for the coach. They all come around and have their good moments. It is a challenge to find the key to make the youngster happy. It is possible that in later life it could well be that the same problem athlete will still have the same personality patterns and have personal relationship problems. However, you can help others appreciate this athlete's strengths, as well as accept their teammate's shortcomings. It can be a good experience for all.

If, however, actions are such that the athlete has negative drag on others, he must change or be let go. A hard worker can get by with some hurts to others because they are respectful of his work and goals and they see a bright side. If, on the other hand, there is lack of work, as well as poor attitude, then everyone is better off parting company. He should undertake something that is rewarding and makes him have a positive outlook rather than being frustrated. Negative thoughts permeate others, and these negative thoughts spread. Rumors that hurt "solidarity" can develop. It is the coach's job to try to make all such thoughts about the future be positive. If you place positive thoughts in your mind or accept only positive thoughts, you tend to create positive outcomes. Dr. Norman V. Peale in his book *Power of Positive Thinking* said it quite well: "Whatever you take into your mind can grow there. Therefore, take the best into your mind and only that. It is a well defined and authentic principle that what the mind profoundly expects it tends to receive." Thus, there is a judgment problem for the coach. You have to help the athlete if it is a worthwhile case; if not, you have to nip it in the bud.

A last thought on dealing with a youngster in severest terms. Assume that you have to let him go. I think it is a much preferable policy to always be friends. Maybe he was just not ready for what he took on. Haven't we all taken on some responsibilities that we underestimated? Be friends, as it pays off for you and for him. What do you gain otherwise? I have had boys come back to the squad after leaving. Many coaches would not entertain any second chances. However, because of good relationships with them, they were ready for a good year after returning. Attitudes were changed and work habits were good. Not everyone is going to be like the coach. Not everyone is going to react like he would want them to. Very few ever return, or would you want them to return, but it is just as easy to be friends.

How many times have you witnessed a coach totally cutting off an athlete after they have parted the coach-athlete relationship? Has it always been justified?

Have you seen problem athletes dealt with too swiftly? Too easily?

State your present philosophy regarding letting a boy return to the team for a second time around.

A VITAL TIME IN PREPARATION FOR SUCCESS

What an athlete does off season is pretty much going to govern his success or failure when the season begins. Special mention needs to be given to this aspect. Once the season begins, it is a race against time, and a lot of what can be accomplished is standard. But improvement time between seasons is vital to the athlete. This is where one can make huge strides. Just imagine a basketball player who loafs during the summer or does something else not related to his game, and compare it to a youngster who shoots an hour a day and plays in a league. He could take a hundred thousand extra shots over the other athlete who did not work at improving. He also has specific conditioning and playing skills to his credit. The same happens in all other sports. The baseball player in college who does not play summer baseball may be pretty much out of it.

If the athlete cannot participate in his sport, he can compete in others to keep his competitive edge. Without this extra work, he loses his advantage when meeting his opponents. Even if he just enjoys conditioning, he is gaining. Off-season conditioning should largely be fun, especially when it is not so concentrated.

The winning and losing edge is often 5 percent or less. And what you do off-season can determine how successful you will be when the regular season begins. The successful athlete has to be an athlete all of the time. You can forget about your sport for brief periods of time, but the athlete at least must be working to make his body develop more cardiorespiratory efficiency, strength, and endurance. Each sport has its own way to achieve this.

Speculate on the potential percentage value of off-season work.

What is an ideal off-season program for your sport?

What are other alternatives for off-season improvement in your sport?

WATCH OUT

Watch out for the natural thing to happen. Youngsters, like the coach and every other human, like to have things going smoothly. It is relaxing. A Saturday win that was a good one often finds the athletes attending practice the next Monday with big grins on their faces. They are happy, and they should be, but it is your job to get them on track again. I will never forget a boy I once had in football. He caught a couple of T.D.s one Saturday, and all week, he acted like life was a bowl of cherries. Nothing could be done to get him to change his attitude. Being a young coach, I probably did not give it the attention I should have. He assumed that good things were always going to happen. *Wrong.* The next Saturday he found out what the cruel world was like—nothing worked—total frustration. It might have been another good day if he had been running scared and was hungry to repeat. The art of harnessing the emotions is vital to the athlete's and team's success. Coaching experience helps tremendously.

A good phrase to remember is, "When things are going good, watch out." Another phrase to remember is, "You'll get a problem just when you don't need one." Athletes often come with a problem at the worst possible time. Run a bit scared and hustle extra hard. Expect problems. Even when you have a couple of extra good practices in a row, watch out for the letdown. If you anticipate and orient your athletes, you will account for fewer problems. Coaching is like tuning a piano—each string must be just right for the concert. To *harness all potential problems* and have everyone on tune is your goal. If this art in coaching could be acquired as a constant, it would be the most sought after quality by those in the field.

At the 1981 National Association for Health Physical Education, Recreation and Dance Convention, Edgar Johnson, University of Delaware swimming coach, brought home this point at a coaching session. Be prepared so that you can cope with Murphy's Law. Murphy's Law states that, "if anything can go wrong, it will." Have a course of planned actions for problems. You'll have enough *unforeseen* problems to challenge your experience and creativity.

What are the typical problems facing a coach?

How can some of these be avoided?

However, let's finish up on a positive note: you are the winner, coach, for all the crises that you meet. Very few occupations can match this opportunity for individual growth. Name one or two if you can.

BIBLIOGRAPHY

Bunn, John: *Scientific Principles of Coaching*. Englewood Cliffs, New Jersey, Prentice-Hall, 1972.

Councilman, James E.: *The Science of Swimming*. Englewood Cliffs, New Jersey, Prentice-Hall, 1968.

Flynn, George L.: *The Vince Lombardi Scrapbook*. A Filmways Company, New York, Grosset and Dunlap Publishers, 1976.

Frost, Reuben B., and Edward J. Sims: *Development of Human Values Through Sports*. Washington, D.C., American Alliance for Health, Physical Education, and Recreation, 1974.

Godfrey, Arthur: I am glad I am alive. *McCalls Magazine, 87*, November, 1959, p. 45.

Grieve, Andrew: Factors influencing a coach's ability to analyze. *Athletic Journal, 51*, June 1971, pp. 42-45, 53-54.

Leggett, Jackson S.: Evaluating your baseball program. *Collegiate Baseball, XXIV, No. 10*, 15 May, 1981, p. 6.

————: Player self-evaluation. *Collegiate Baseball, XXV, No. 11*, 15 June, 1981.

Peale, Norman V.: *The Power of Positive Thinking*. Englewood Cliffs, New Jersey, Prentice-Hall, 1956.

Veller, Donald.: Get the right boy in the right job. *Athletic Journal, 46*, March 1966, pp. 46-54, 85-87.